The List

The List

7 WAYS TO TELL IF HE'S GOING TO MARRY YOU— IN 30 DAYS OR LESS!

Mary Corbett and Sheila Corbett Kihne

ADAMS MEDIA

Avon, Massachusetts

Published by Adams Media, an F+W Publications Company
57 Littlefield Street, Avon, MA 02322
www.adamsmedia.com.

ISBN: 1-59337-400-3

Printed in Canada

J I H G F E D C B

Library of Congress Cataloging-in-Publication Data
Corbett, Mary.
The list : 7 ways to tell if he's going to marry you—in 30 days
or less! / Mary Corbett and Sheila Corbett Kihne.
         p.   cm.
ISBN 1-59337-400-3
1. Mate selection. 2. Man-woman relationships.
3. Single women. I. Kihne, Sheila Corbett. II. Title.
HQ801.C7195 2005
646.7'7—dc22
2005002136

This publication is designed to provide accurate and authoritative information with regard to the subject matter covered. It is sold with the understanding that the publisher is not engaged in rendering legal, accounting, or other professional advice. If legal advice or other expert assistance is required, the services of a competent professional person should be sought.

    —From a *Declaration of Principles* jointly adopted by a Committee of the American Bar Association and a Committee of Publishers and Associations

Many of the designations used by manufacturers and sellers to distinguish their products are claimed as trademarks. Where those designations appear in this book and Adams Media was aware of a trademark claim, the designations have been printed with initial capital letters.

This book is available at quantity discounts for bulk purchases.
For information, please call 1-800-872-5627.

Dedication

This book is fondly dedicated to Jon, Todd, and all the men in the "Good Husband Club" who helped inspire *The List*. They're the real men, the heroes, the gentlemen, the grand prizes in the game of love. We wrote this book to give them the recognition that they deserve.

CONTENTS

Acknowledgments

First, we really need to thank our terrible former bosses. If it weren't for you (and you know who you are) we wouldn't have quit our jobs and started this book. What's your problem, anyway? Sure, we weren't perfect employees but we weren't *that* bad.

Kidding aside, one person, in particular, deserves our warmest thanks. Gail Johnson gave us the momentum to keep the project going when we were ready to put it aside. Gail has been a dear friend for nearly twenty-five years. And when we were frustrated and creatively "blocked," we knew that Gail would tell us what to do. It didn't matter that she had a busy job or that she was chasing after two children (one who was undergoing treatment for leukemia); Gail knew we needed her and she came through—like she always does! Gail passed our thin little manuscript around to all the single ladies in her office and even made a copy for her husband, Larry. She collected everybody's feedback and sent our copies back with helpful notes in the margins. Most importantly she said, "Everybody loved it. I think you are going to make your living as writers." Gail's good opinion was all we needed to keep writing. Thanks, Wookie!

Big thanks also to family members, Don and Lucy Corbett, Anne and Tom Forbes, Tom and Daphne Corbett, Frances Melby Thomas, Elizabeth Melby Wells, Anita, Stephen, Jodi, Mike and Darlene Kihne, and Roscoe for their constant support and enthusiasm. We also appreciate the friends who always ask us, "What's going on with the book?" (though they are probably tired of hearing about it!). This group includes: Linda Saggau, Tina Eyerly, Lynn Draper,

Tricia Feagin, Kim Carlyle, Monica Williams, Ginny Haynie, Stephanie Butler, Lea Brueckner, and Deborah Enea. We also want to thank all of the couples who shared their stories with us.

Finally, thanks to our agent Evelyn Fazio and the Adams Media team of Gary M. Krebs, Danielle Chiotti, and Bridget Brace. You took a chance on us and really put your arms around this project. Thanks for believing in us and believing in *The List*.

NOTE TO READERS

Single men are hereby put on notice: Only the strong shall survive.

Welcome to *The List* Revolution, ladies. From this point on, your life will never be the same. Women all over the country are telling men, "I'm sorry, Chuck-o, but you waited three days to call me. I'm not interested."

It's time to put the onus back where it belongs: squarely on a man's strong shoulders. You don't need to manage your heart like a business, track men like they were sales leads, or wait around to become the victim of a breakup—just reassess the way you have dated in the past, and stop wasting time with men who are not going to marry you.

If you choose to only date men who do the things on *The List* and to dump the men who cannot perform the actions on *The List*, you will never have your heart broken again . . . and you will find a man who loves you and wants to marry you.

HOW

The LISt

CAME TO BE

Sheila's Fairy Tale

My dating experiences began during high school, when I was a sophomore. Our entire class paired off and I was "lucky" enough to be asked out by a good-looking senior baseball player who drove a late-model Camaro. He was charming and attentive and even scared off any other potential suitors with threats of physical violence. How flattering!

When he left to attend a nearby college, he insisted that we remain boyfriend and girlfriend, even though I had doubts. In hindsight, it is obvious that he was dating other girls but still wanted to keep me locked up for his Friday night date. I wasted two years on this silly, stupid relationship. Finally, he dumped me by driving to my parents' house and taking me for a walk while his friend waited in the car. I ran home in tears, humiliated, and never talked to him again.

I had parents who had instilled in me the belief that I could do anything I wanted to do, and I was pretty successful at that point in my young life—yet I still got trapped in a bad relationship. I vowed to myself that I would never, ever let any man embarrass me like that again, and I stayed true to that promise. At the ripe old age of seventeen, I had learned a valuable lesson that would eventually lead me to happiness.

I spent the first two years of college casually dating. I never had a problem attracting guys. I still had minor problems with early detection of losers, burnouts, and pompous jerks. But it was college! Who expects to meet a nice, respectful guy in college, anyway?

Then I met Todd.

Todd was the first guy who walked right up to me and introduced himself. It was during my sorority sister's rowdy twenty-first-birthday bar-hopping party.

"Hi, my name is Todd; you look like you're having a good time. What's your name?"

There was none of that BS of telling someone else to tell me that he thought I was cute or staring at me across the room until I approached him, or sliding next to me to comment about the tequila shots being downed at the bar.

I had never been approached in such a direct, polite way. I was friendly to Todd, and let him buy me a beer. I then spent the rest of the night dancing on tables and singing obnoxiously at the piano bar with a large group of girlfriends.

After our first meeting, Todd immediately asked a mutual friend about my dating status and called me right away. I thought pretty quickly that Todd was cute, kind, very funny, and intelligent, but my defense mechanisms were up and I was scared to death. I told myself that I was young—way too young—to get involved with anyone seriously. I didn't want to get hurt again, and it really freaked me out to have this nice guy pursue me for just being me.

Thank goodness for the green-eyed monster. It was only when I saw him at a party dancing with a girl whom I could not stand that I realized how I felt. Isn't it silly when a woman only thinks a man is worth something if another woman wants him? I immediately cut in, and that was it. We have been inseparable from that moment on. If that one moment had not happened, who knows where I'd be right now. After twelve years of knowing and loving Todd, I can't imagine my life without him.

But, I'll give myself some credit. I knew in my heart that I wanted a family, stability, and a man who truly loved me. I had enough sense to realize that Todd was the man who could give me all of these things. And I loved him. So even though marrying him would mean I had to sideline dreams of moving to Washington, D.C., I knew what I had to do.

I remember the moment I made up my mind like it was yesterday. I was sitting in my sorority bedroom when it just hit me: If I don't marry Todd, he will find someone else and I'll be making the biggest mistake of my life.

I'm not sure how I had that wisdom at twenty-one. Perhaps it was the lesson of the bad high school relationship, or maybe it was pure luck. I believe it was divine intervention.

I chose to ignore the messages from society that women should not marry young. I mean, you're practically a hillbilly if you're married in your early twenties in this country! People asked me things like: "Don't you want to pursue your career first?" "Why don't you just keep dating?" "I never pictured you getting married so young. Aren't you afraid you're sacrificing your success for him?"

For me, marriage actually became a secret weapon in the working world. As a married woman, I was immediately considered more mature, more responsible, and more stable. I had something in common with older colleagues and customers. I believe this, at least in part, led to my career success at a young age. Some people say that if you marry young, you will never know if there is someone "better" out there. If you meet a man who loves you, respects you, and treats you well, how could you meet someone better?

Todd and I figured that there wasn't any reason to postpone marriage; we wanted to start building a future together immediately. Time flies by so quickly, so in the grand scheme of things, what is the difference between getting married at twenty-two or twenty-eight? If a man is going to marry you, he will want to do it as soon as he reasonably can. For Todd and me, this meant getting married right after my graduation.

Our marriage has its good stretches and bad stretches, like anyone else's. But we're both happy with where we are in life. We make each other laugh a lot. We love talking politics, and we enjoy just sitting together and watching television. He is truly my best friend and my soul mate.

If you had a Todd in your life and you let him go, then by all means, call him up and see if he's still single. If not, you've got to start at the beginning. Read with an open mind and adopt *The List* as your guidebook. If you do, you will find your other half. Oh, and please invite me to the wedding . . . I love a good party!

Mary's Fairy Tale

Eleven years ago, when I was twenty-six years old, I walked down the aisle toward the wrong man. Doesn't sound like anyone's classic Fairy Tale, does it? But the thing about a Fairy Tale is that the only thing that matters is the ending. There are many paths that lead to "happily ever after."

For as long as I can remember, I have attracted nice guys. But I was never interested in them. Like many women, I felt that any man worth having was worth chasing. I really didn't date much in high school. I had a wonderful group of friends, and a boyfriend wasn't a "must-have."

Once I left my safety net to go to college, however, things changed. I felt a little insecure about being totally on my own in four years. I would have to make my own money and go into the world by myself. I thought it would be so much easier to have a man by my side. Many of the girls I met my freshman year hooked up with serious boyfriends right out of the gate. I thought they had the leg up. Rather than date the "friend" who adored me, I ran up and down Greek row with my big hair and small standards. After a couple of failed attempts at couplehood, I set my sights on a man who would play mind games with me, cheat on me, and destroy my self-confidence. I wasted my junior and senior year on an emotional roller coaster, pining after him. After college, I moved to New York City, made friends fast, and dated a lot of different men. But I made all of the same mistakes that I had made in college. I blew off the nice guys and spent my energy on the men who weren't interested in me.

When I moved back to Minnesota a few years later, I decided that I had had enough and was going to get married. I met a man who was nine years older than I was. He was stable and nice and had a lot going for him, but we were completely incompatible. I knew this on some level, but all of my friends were getting married and I panicked. I issued quite a few ultimatums, and we got married.

Almost immediately after getting married, I knew that I had made a mistake. I was between a rock and a hard place: I knew that the marriage wasn't working, but I didn't want to start over. What if I ended up alone? I decided to put on a happy face. I focused all of my energy on my job as a marketing manager at the hottest architecture firm in

Minneapolis. I made cool new friends, worked long hours, and lived in the fast lane. Things changed when I was offered and accepted a position as director at a quiet, stodgy design firm that needed some youthful energy.

Each and every one of the partners at my new firm had been happily married to the same woman for decades. When they talked about their wives and their kids, their sweet cherubic faces lit up. Working there changed me forever.

Some days, I would go into my office and shut the door and cry. I felt like my personal life was in shambles. Finally, I decided that I needed to get a handle on things. My professional life was in great shape. I wanted my personal life to be on a par. Either I was going to have the Fairy Tale or I would be alone. Either way, I would be okay.

I got a divorce. Over the next two years, I continued in therapy. I figured out why I had such a warped notion of love, rediscovered what made me happy, and realized that even though I wanted to have love in my life, I couldn't really control that. The only thing I could do was to be the best person I could be and put myself out there.

And boy did I get out there. Although I spent quality time with my friends, I really became my own best friend. I went on long walks with my dog, bought my own home, excelled at work, joined a playwright's center, planned a fundraiser for a photography gallery, hung out at my favorite coffee shop, wrote a musical about historic preservation, and went to mass every Sunday. (Whew!) It wasn't easy doing all of these things by myself, but I did it just the same. I was alone, but I wasn't lonely.

And eventually, I felt like Mary again. Not the Mary who chased men and tried to make them love her, but the Mary who loved herself. All of the wasted years just disappeared. It was at this point that I knew that I was ready for love—real love—to find me. But I was thirty-one years old, and I knew that I didn't have time to waste.

Since I had decided that I could handle being alone, I used dating as an opportunity to really pay attention to how different men acted in the early stages of dating. I noticed certain red-flag behaviors that helped identify the men who really weren't interested in anything serious. If a man slipped up in the slightest way, I dumped him flat.

Of course I would get tricked from time to time, but I never made the same mistake twice.

And on a day like any other day, everything changed. I attended a neighborhood meeting to discuss the fate of an old movie theater. Little did I know my prince was there.

Jon was one of 200-plus people attending the meeting. I didn't see him. A quick scan of the room showed that most of the people there were retirees with nothing to do but argue in public. I spoke my piece and made a quick exit. Three days later, a card arrived in the mail from a secret admirer. This person was at the meeting and liked what I had to say. He wanted to take me out to breakfast. I was flattered but scared. What kind of a guy would go to such trouble?

And he did go to a lot of trouble. I found out later that when I introduced myself before speaking, Jon quickly jotted down my name. But he got it wrong. He thought it was Corbin. He recruited his friends to find me. And a couple of days later, his Internet-savvy friend found a Mary Corbett who lived in the neighborhood. Jon did several "drive-bys" to see if the woman living at that address matched the woman he had seen. Finally, he decided to send me a card.

That weekend, my two gay friends came to check out my new house. They sat at my dining room table swilling down Heineken and teasing me because I didn't have a boyfriend or a stereo. I brought out the card. They insisted that I invite "Stalker" over for a drink. I picked up the phone, chatted with him briefly, and greeted him at the door an hour later.

Stalker was carrying a stereo in one arm and a bottle of pinot grigio in another.

"Hi, I'm Jon," he said, reaching for my hand.

And the expression on his face! He looked like a little kid who had walked into his own surprise party, a big nervous grin on his face and bright, hopeful blue eyes.

He set up the stereo as my friends eyed him suspiciously. I went into the kitchen to get him a glass of wine. I could hear that he was holding his own with the rainbow firing squad and smiled to myself.

I enjoyed the evening. I didn't try to impress him. I figured "so far, so good" and just stayed in the moment. The next afternoon after returning home from a baby shower, I found a note on my front door asking me to dinner that night. I had plans that I couldn't break and figured if he was really interested, he would be persistent. And he was. Before I could even pick up the phone to tell him that I was busy, he had already phoned me to follow up. He made a date for the very next morning.

I met him at our neighborhood coffee shop. It was just a casual date but the sparks flew. I felt something that I had never felt before. It was something bigger than love. I felt like everything that I had done in my life was meant to bring me to this moment. I felt peace. That was it. Ten days later we were engaged.

Jon had every reason to postpone the engagement. He didn't have a ton of money. He still hadn't finished his degree. Hell, he barely knew me. The only thing he knew was that he wanted me to be his wife. One night, we drove to the jewelry store and put a beautiful oval-cut diamond ring on his charge card. I was married shortly after my thirty-second birthday.

I couldn't believe it. After years of hearing about the Fairy Tale, it had finally happened to *me*. And in the years since, I am amazed that other happily married couples share similar stories. For every married couple that spent years playing games and trading ultimatums, there is a happily married couple that had a Fairy Tale courtship.

Of course, our marriage isn't perfect, but we are still deeply and madly in love with each other. When we have a "bad marriage day" (which all couples do), I remember how we met and can't help but smile.

It took a few solid years of focus and faith to transform myself from a woman who needed a man—any man—to make her feel loved into a woman who would rather be alone than settle for anything less than a prince. Every woman deserves to be pursued and won over. That's what *The List* is all about.

Fairy Tales do come true. Believe!

The List *Is Born*

From the outside looking in, we are two very different women who took two very different paths to true love.

▷ Sheila met Todd when she was a sophomore in college. Sheila is very organized and particular. She likes English antiques and toile. She married Todd and built a successful career in sales while he pursued his medical career. She and Todd "grew up together" in many ways.

▷ Mary was divorced and over thirty when she met Jon. She is creative and a little "out there." She likes modern, simple things. She built a successful career in the architectural field on her own. She and Jon both had their own homes, careers, and social circles when their paths crossed.

Not only are we very different, our husbands are very different too:

▷ Sheila's husband, Todd, is a shy, thoughtful doctor who has excelled at everything he has ever attempted.

▷ Mary's husband, Jon, is an opinionated and hilarious U.S. Army officer who took an unconventional path to career success.

▷ One was twenty-four when he proposed, the other thirty-one. One was the son of a physician who took annual ski trips, the other the son of a cop who lived on a hobby farm and rode horses.

Everything about our Fairy Tales is night and day except one thing: Our husbands did the exact same things during courtship. There were no games, no rules, and no gimmicks. They made it easy for us.

Were we the only ones out there who experienced this kind of courtship? Was it supposed to be more dramatic and drawn out? Were we crazy for latching on so soon? We decided to compare notes. Whenever we met a new couple, we asked them how they met and when they "knew." The stories from happily married people started to sound strikingly similar. Each couple remembered being almost instantly "inseparable." Each couple remembered a natural, easy, and swift journey toward the altar. Ashley, a woman who met and married her husband within four months, describes it this way:

"The potential of marriage was what was driving our relationship. I wrote in my journal that our relationship felt like a snowball rolling down a hill . . . it kept getting bigger and bigger, and I couldn't stop it if I wanted to."

We compared all of the stories we had collected with a story that we already knew well: the story of how our own parents met. Mom was a nice girl from a nice family in Minneapolis. Her life was very sheltered. Dad was from a very, shall we say, "energetic" Bronx family. His mother died when he was thirteen and he was wise beyond his years. He had moved to Minnesota to attend college. One weekend, Mom went to visit her older brother at St. John's University. She was dancing with another man when Dad cut in. They talked, and he was hooked. He followed up their first meeting by writing her a letter stating when he was going to pick her up for their first official date. Unfortunately, he had the wrong address and the letter was delivered to a neighbor's house. Regardless of the mix-up, he still showed up on my mother's doorstep.

"Don asked me to marry him one month after we met. I was only eighteen and I knew that my parents would be upset. I put him off

and said we needed time, and we continued to date exclusively. He graduated in May and really turned up the heat that summer. By this time I knew I loved him and that he was very dedicated to me—who could ask for more? We were engaged in January and married in September."

Forty years later, our grandmother is still recovering from the shock. Mom can relate every detail of their whirlwind courtship. Dad simply says:

"I saw her, I was ready, and that was it."

Dad's statement is to courtship what Einstein's theory of relativity is to physics. It is that big, yet that simple: *"I saw her, I was ready, and that was it."*

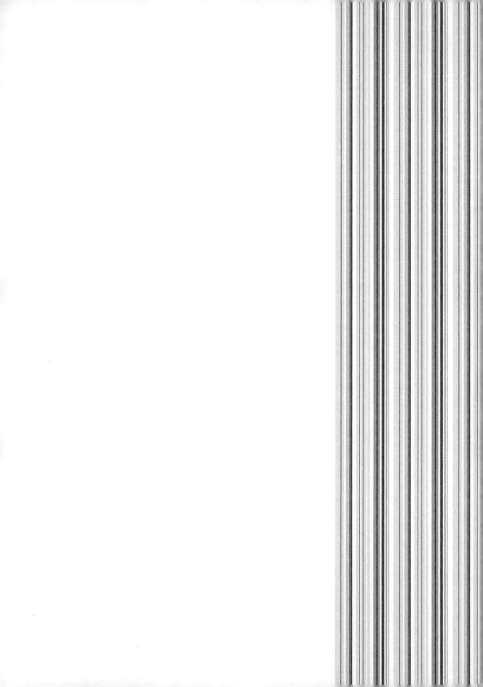

ONE

HOW TO USE

The **List**

The Alarm

To understand why *The List* works, you first have to fully comprehend The Alarm. Pay attention: We're telling you something about men that they don't even know about themselves. There is an Alarm built into every man that he doesn't even know exists. When a man meets the woman he is going to marry, The Alarm sounds loudly. He has never heard this sound before. But instinctively, he knows what he needs to do. He has to win this woman's heart before anybody else gets to her.

To secure her heart and her hand, he will do seven things. These actions make up *The List*:

1. He makes the first move.
2. He calls you within twenty-four to forty-eight hours to set up a first date.
3. He makes the first date easy and fun.
4. He calls you within twenty-four hours to set up subsequent dates—they are easy, fun, and one-on-one.
5. He wants to talk to you every day and wants to spend all his free time with you.
6. He demonstrates unconditional loyalty.
7. He talks about marrying you in concrete terms and proposes—or lets you know his intentions.

Believe it or not, *all of these actions will occur within thirty days.* He may have been a pig the week before—he may be a happy bachelor not even thinking of marriage—but when this man meets the right woman, he becomes a List Man. All of a sudden the only thing that matters is getting close to the woman of his dreams. It becomes like breathing to him.

Sid, a happily married man who proposed to his wife within a month, shared this story:

"Years before I met Tricia, a man I respected—and a fifty-year veteran of marriage—told me that a man knows within two to three dates if he is going to marry a woman. He was right."

Spoken like a true List Man.

The Alarm sounds only when a million different aspects of a woman are perfectly in synch with a man. He may have approached you. He may have asked you out. He may have taken you on the best date(s) of your life. He may think you are really attractive and like your personality. He may even be your boyfriend. None of these things mean that you have sounded The Alarm. Checking off every item on *The List* is the only true measure.

Understanding how The Alarm works is the key to *The List*. If you don't understand The Alarm, you will waste time hoping that a marriage proposal is imminent when it isn't even a possibility. You will think there is something wrong with you. Or you will convince yourself that he will eventually come around. You will make excuses and try to fix something that can't be fixed.

When you meet a man and sound his Alarm, everything will fall into place quickly. You won't have to worry, wait, or wonder. *The List* quantifies what a happily married woman means when she says, "You just know" when asked about meeting her husband. *The List* breaks an abstract idea down into measurable actions.

Control What You Can Control

Any good twelve-step program will tell you to "accept the things you cannot change and have the courage to change the things you can." Since you can't change or control The Alarm, focus your attention on the only thing you can control: how you react when you don't sound The Alarm.

Don't be devastated if you haven't sounded The Alarm. After all, it has nothing to do with you. Feel relieved that you have correctly diagnosed the problem and don't have to waste time on a lost cause. You will never have to waste time wondering what it means when a man says things like "What's the hurry?" Or when he talks about marriage in vague terms, like, "Yeah, I can see getting married someday." Or when he says to his girlfriend of two years, "I love you and want to marry you, but I just need a little time."

When a man says such things, it means you haven't sounded The Alarm, and that means that his time is up, baby. With *The List*, men will no longer have the advantage of choosing from a pool of women who accept these tired delay tactics.

You are a wonderful woman (everybody says so!) and you deserve to be pursued by a man who loves you and wants to marry you more than anything in the world. Now that you have *The List*, you will never have your wonderful heart broken again. You won't have to do anything but relax and be yourself. Then judge a man's actions against *The List*. If he does the things on *The List*, proceed with confidence. If he falters at all, let him see the back of you.

"Woman Math"

If you're like most women, you've done the "woman math" in your head to determine when you want to get married. Here's an example:

> *"I want to have my first child by the time I'm thirty-three. It will take a year to have the baby and up to a year to get pregnant, and we'd want to spend a year alone, so that means I need to be married by age thirty. So I'll need to be engaged by the time I'm twenty-nine. That gives us a year to be engaged and find a place to have the wedding. Which means I'll need to find a boyfriend by the time I'm twenty-six since we'll need to date for at least a couple of years . . . Blah, blah, blah."*

In a million years, Sheila never would have dreamed that she was going to get married at the tender age of twenty-two. But she did. And she had to adjust her calendar accordingly.

When Mary graduated from high school in 1985, she never would have guessed that it would take her sixteen years to have her first child. But it did. And to get to that point in her life, she had to change her calculations several times.

But did Todd and Jon think about these things? Do any men think like this? Hell *no* they don't. They can't think like this. Only women could be so sensible. And only women have biological clocks.

Most women think about this timeline before they even meet their Prince Charming (or frog, as the case might be). The reason we are so tuned in to numbers is because we know a couple things deep inside:

▷ A woman's prime dating lifespan is from age twenty to thirty.
▷ A man's prime dating lifespan is from age twenty to forty.

For a woman, we define "prime" as the window of opportunity in which the following things are true:

1. She is able to have her pick of the crop without major competition from younger women.
2. She isn't feeling panicked by her biological clock.
3. She has the widest possible selection of men to choose from who are in her age range.
4. There is absolutely no societal scrutiny regarding her single status.

Even a woman in a hurry to get married knows that a man may not be. We all have seen a lot of couples date for years before getting married. It's perfectly acceptable for a man to marry in his forties and still be able to "have it all."

"Man Math"

There is no "man math." Men are different from women in this regard. First the man has to meet the right woman, and *then* he starts thinking about marriage. A man doesn't start plotting his future when he is twenty-two or even thirty. He starts plotting his future when The Alarm sounds. Remember: *"I saw her, I was ready, and that was it."*

When The Alarm sounds he is only thinking about getting near this woman and finding out why he is so madly attracted to her.

After he gets to know her a little bit, The Alarm continues to guide him. He loses his sense of practicality and will overcome any obstacle to be with her. He won't give a hoot about numbers or timelines. He won't care how old he is or how old she is. He won't care if his job is moving him across the country in three months. He won't care when he finds out that she wants to get engaged after only a month or two. He won't care if he doesn't have any money in the bank. He will do whatever it takes to close the deal. There is no "man math." There is no "man timeline." There is only The Alarm.

Furthermore, during courtship, there is no discussion of math at all. A List Man doesn't talk numbers of any kind when he is courting you. Things having to do with numbers include, but are not limited to, practical matters like these:

- Money
- Salary
- Mileage
- Calendars
- Clocks
- Schedules
- Timelines
- Weight
- Age

The only number a List Man is interested in is your phone number. Numbers are boring, and they are usually associated with something rigid. He doesn't want to be rigid with you. He wants to be relaxed and reliable. If you have sounded The Alarm, he wants to keep everything light and fun so he can secure your heart and hand. He will have fifty years to hound you about your credit card balance. Why would he risk scaring you away by saying anything related to numbers, like:

- ▷ "Well, it's getting late, and I have a big day tomorrow. Gotta go."
- ▷ "I'm going out of town for two weeks."
- ▷ "Chocolate cake? I thought you were on a diet!"
- ▷ "Sorry I didn't call. I was at the office until ten P.M."
- ▷ "Your half of the tab is $37.50."
- ▷ "Wow. I didn't realize this place was so expensive."
- ▷ "Well, it's kind of a long drive. Why don't we just see each other tomorrow?"
- ▷ "I've only been with the firm six weeks so I'm really limited for time right now."
- ▷ "I'm trying to save money."
- ▷ "Since the company is paying, I'm going to stay a couple of extra days."
- ▷ "Most of the women I've dated are younger."

If a man is talking math with you, he is dating you not courting you.

If You Force a Man to Talk about "Woman Math," He Will Win Every Time

When a woman hasn't sounded The Alarm, she will fear for her timeline. And rightly so! She will start to calculate her current situation according to her woman math. She will become fixated with things like "six-month dating" anniversaries and make these occasions seem like milestones. She will bring up timelines for engagement and ask to know where she stands. She wants to give him the message, "I'm counting." When a man's Alarm hasn't sounded, he dreads discussing woman math. It puts him off his game. When a woman brings up timelines, he knows that he is being stalked and something in his "Ug the Hunter" makeup realizes that there is something wrong with this scenario. It's the same thing that makes him balk at a used-car dealership. It's the same thing that makes the card shark in Vegas decide to fold and not call. It's the voice in his head that says, "Just walk away."

The Stall

And what is the modern, caring, sensitive male's version of this? It's The Stall. This boyfriend you want to be with forever and ever is not the brave, gritty hero you want him to be. He doesn't want to give up anything. He wants to have all the benefits of a committed relationship without any of the responsibility. So he uses The Stall.

A woman brings up the timeline in what she believes is a very factual and sensible way. He will feel cornered and respond by saying things that she can't argue with or things that will placate her. Do any of these lines sound familiar?

▷ "We've only been dating for [fill in months or years], what's the hurry?"

- ▷ "Sure I want to get married … someday."
- ▷ "Maybe in another six months we can get engaged."
- ▷ "You know I love you. I just need more time."
- ▷ "As soon as I … finish my MBA … get more money in the bank … buy a house … get promoted at work … we can talk about getting married."
- ▷ "I want to have enough money for a [big ring, big wedding, big house], so let's just hold off for a while."
- ▷ "I'm ready for the next step. Let's move in together."

With lines like these, it is no wonder a man can accomplish The Stall so easily. He remains cool and collected and makes the woman think that his future plans include her, and that's how he wins every time. A woman will disregard sound advice and go against her own intuition because it all seems so believable. Why? Because she *wants* to believe it. What a woman hears is "I'm going to marry you when the time is right." But what the man is actually saying is "I'm not sure." Obviously, there is no rush for him. Why would he rush to marry somebody who hasn't sounded The Alarm? He knows that the woman isn't going to leave him, so he chooses the path of least confrontation. The Stall is a man's best friend when he is cornered because the only thing he needs to do is buy a little time. He will make excuses. He will make promises. He will say whatever it takes to calm the Huntress.

Always remember that if you have sounded The Alarm, you won't fear for your timeline and bring up woman math. You won't have to hunt and become a victim of The Stall. You won't have to worry about anything. All of the actions will be his responsibility. He will do the things on *The List* and take cues from you to figure out what you want. If you want a proposal, he will produce a proposal. Then, he will sit back and relax (boy, will he relax—but that's another book) because he knows that he has you. And he knows that you are happy with him.

Redo the Math and Reset the Clock

If you are going to use *The List*, you need a clean slate. *The List* is powerful, but it can't change the outlook of an ill-fated relationship.

Regardless of whether you are in a long-term relationship or just in the beginning stages of dating, if a man hasn't done the things on *The List*, it is time to redo the math and reset the clock. Take the emotions out of it. You thought you may have sounded The Alarm, but you didn't. It's happened to everybody. Every woman we know has had her heart broken by wasting time on the wrong man. Those women who claim they haven't, well, they're just liars!

Some women prefer to continue making the same mistakes over and over again rather than adopt a new way of looking at things. They usually end up single. Other women decide that they are going to get what they want no matter how bumpy the road is. They are willing to believe in *The List* and make a new start. They usually end up married.

The List makes it simple to see things clearly and *The List* provides real "proof" that a particular man isn't going to marry you. If you are a woman out in the dating world, you won't pin your hopes on the wrong men. Never again will you think things are going well when they really aren't. If you have been out with a man a few times but feel his interest is waning, you can give him the pink slip without worrying that you are walking away from a potential mate. If your long-term boyfriend hasn't proposed, and the two of you have no concrete plans for marriage, you will realize that The Alarm never sounded and there isn't anything that you can do to close the deal. No matter what situation you are in, your chances of getting married are much higher if you start anew. The sooner you walk away, the sooner you will get married. It is likely that in a year or two, you will be married to a man you haven't even met yet! Don't worry about your timeline, with *The List*, you can make up for lost time.

If you stay in a dead-end relationship, odds are that you will not be married within a year or two. Or, worse yet, you may convince him to marry you and end up in an ill-fated marriage. In married life, you'll deal with the same problems you had while you were dating. His true feelings toward you won't change. If he doesn't spend enough time with you, doesn't give you the emotional support you need, or thinks you are too needy, that will not change with marriage. You will have twice as much laundry to do and the lion's share of child care on your plate, but you won't suddenly get more from him. And if you end up getting divorced, you really will have a timeline mess (not to mention a billion other emotional strains and issues) on your hands.

When Exes Come Back

If you are reading this book to get your head back in the game after you've been dumped by a man, be warned that he may (and most likely will) come back to you with his tail between his legs. More often than not, his reappearance will coincide with your recovery. It happens all the time. Just when a woman is finally feeling confident again, her old boyfriend comes back into the picture. He tells her everything she wanted to hear while they were dating:

> ▷ "You were the best girlfriend; I don't know what I was thinking."
> ▷ "I miss you so much."
> ▷ "I can't see myself without you."
> ▷ "I realized how much I love you."

Sometimes, he will even say the big one:

> ▷ "I'm ready to get married."

Don't fool yourself into thinking that this is how things are "meant to be" or that this is really romantic. What is romantic about somebody dumping you flat and then coming back to you because he is bored, lonely, or scared of the future? Also, please note that nobody else was interested in his pathetic little self. It's no wonder. Having buyer's remorse over an oxford shirt or a dinner entrée is understandable, but over a woman? Come on.

If an ex does come back in this way, consider it the ultimate blessing. He has given the power back to you to say something like:

> ▷ "I'm really not interested in seeing you again."
> ▷ "I've moved on, and I don't want to go back to that time in my life."
> ▷ "I'm glad you broke up with me, because what we had was really awful, don't you think?"

Or, *you* may be able to say the big one:

▷ "I'm getting married."

If a guy dumped you once, it means that you didn't sound his Alarm the first time you dated. His wanting you back doesn't change that. If you haven't sounded his Alarm yet, you never will. Don't be fooled again. Even if this lesser man does propose, you will have a lackluster marriage rooted in the fact that he had already rejected you before you even walked down the aisle.

If you keep doing the same thing, you will get the same results. For *The List* to work, you need to start your journey with a clean slate and a new attitude. The past is water under the bridge. Don't waste any more time! Brush yourself off and get to work. Set a new goal: *No more roller-coaster relationships; no more wasted time.*

By identifying the actions a man will take if he is going to marry you and measuring these actions in the order they occur, you can start fresh with the guarantee that you will never suffer a fool again. You are in control of your goal. Just complete this thought:

"I am ___ years old. My goal is to be married by the time I am ___ years old. To do this, I will clean my current slate because if I don't, I won't meet my goal. I will use The List *to assess a man's intentions as quickly as possible. I will clean my slate as many times as it takes to meet the man of my dreams. The man of my dreams will do all the things on* The List *because I will have sounded his Alarm."*

Do you see how simple it is? Do you see how much better it is to set a new goal rather than cling to an old hope? Don't ever sell yourself short again.

That's how *The List* works!

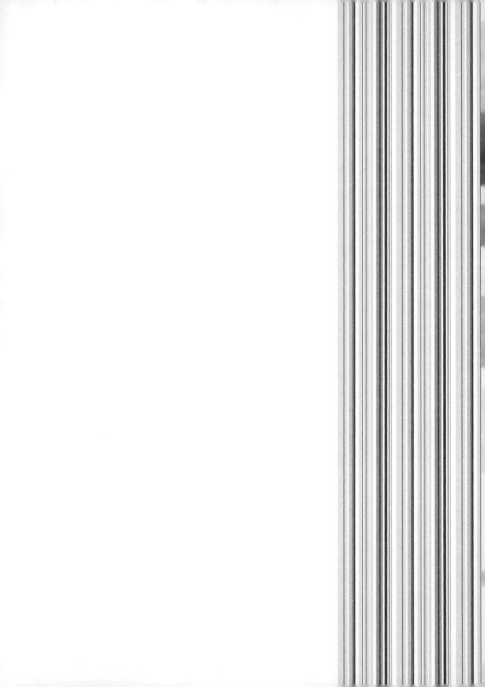

TWO

Operation
FAIRY TALE

LET'S
GET TO WORK

Know What You Are Looking For

If *The List* is going to work, you need to realize that a man should be judged on his actions and how they affect you. Many women judge the wrong things in dating. They pick apart perfectly nice men, and the only guys they think are good enough for them (ironically) are the ones who aren't interested in them.

If you want *The List* to work for you, you need to know what is truly important in life. Life is about surrounding yourself with people you love and who love you back unconditionally, forever. Your spouse should top that list.

Finding the right mate is the most important thing you will ever do. If you are worried about what your friends will think about your partner, then you probably need new friends. People who truly love you and have your best interests at heart will adore anybody who adores you.

Years before meeting Jon, Mary sat down with her best friend Gail, and the two wrote down an "off the top of your head" accounting of what Mary wanted in her future husband. Really, the requirements were simple:

- ▷ Only has eyes for me
- ▷ Supports me and loves me as I am
- ▷ Mutual physical attraction
- ▷ Wants to have kids someday
- ▷ Great sense of humor
- ▷ Honest and honorable
- ▷ Confident

> ▷ Likes to be with me all the time
> ▷ Has same values

Mary carried this note in her wallet for three years. When she finally met Jon, she knew he had the things that she wanted.

To attract a good man, you need to keep an open mind while staying true to your own values. List Men are attracted to women who have a keen sense of self. You should be able to articulate and stay true to your own values. To make sure that you aren't being too picky—or too accommodating—make a table. Title the left column "Things He Must Have" and the right column "Things That Would Be Nice to Have." Think about the things you want your List Man to have and the places where you won't settle for less. Then think of things that would be nice but maybe aren't as necessary.

Does your table look something like this?

THINGS HE MUST HAVE	THINGS THAT WOULD BE NICE TO HAVE
Only has eyes for me	Great looking
Sense of humor	Great intellectual
Supports me constantly	Amazing wardrobe
Loves me for who I am	Loves to travel
Doesn't criticize me	Buff body
Has good work ethic	Prestigious profession
Responsible with money	Has a lot of money
Honest and trustworthy	Never been married
Wants kids; will be a good father	No children from previous marriage
Similar views on politics/religion	Highly educated

THINGS HE MUST HAVE	THINGS THAT WOULD BE NICE TO HAVE
Strong attraction	Full head of hair
Likes to spend time with me	Perfect teeth
Gets along with others	Comes from a great family
No harmful addictions	Nice Car
Wants to marry me	Unfailingly romantic

Notice how the things in the "Must Have" column are pretty big picture, while a lot of the things in the "Nice to Have" column seem pretty shallow and ridiculous. Think about all of the failed romances that you have had, and ask yourself why they failed. You're probably going to find common denominators. Maybe you are attracted to men involved in prestigious professions. But if you had a relationship with a businessman who worked late every night and on weekends and you don't like to be alone, you need to reassess what you really want. Or maybe you are only interested in great-looking men. But if you are insecure and need a lot of reassurance from the man in your life, perfect looks are not what you need in a mate. Perhaps you would never, ever consider dating a blue-collar man or a man without a college degree. But if he treats you well and has a great work ethic, why would you ditch him for someone with an M.B.A. who treats you poorly?

Just remember that your "Must Haves" are fixed—you won't take anything less than what you know you need in a man. Sometimes women get so excited about a man that they make the mistake of adopting his values and forgetting about their own. With *The List*, you can be who you are and be true to what you need and value. You won't need to adopt his political views. You won't have to pretend that he doesn't drink too much when he does. You won't need to say you don't want kids if you really do. You won't have to pretend that living together is fine when marriage is what you want. It's when The Alarm hasn't sounded that you will be tempted to compromise what is important to you. Remember, when a man is courting you, he will love you for who you are because The Alarm has gone off.

We are happy to report that if a man has all your "Must Haves," there is nothing wrong with him—so don't fixate on some of the other things you *wish* he had. The delicious truth is that a List Man loves you the way that you are, but he is willing to let you make him a bit of a project! We are women, after all. A man who loves you will admire your taste and judgment and is likely to take your well-intended suggestions in stride.

He can finish his degree after you are married. If he has twenty pounds to lose but has everything else you want, then start working out together. Chances are that he will want to be as attractive as possible for you and will volunteer to improve himself in any way necessary. Just don't rule out anybody before you give him a chance.

At age thirty-three, Laura, a very pretty and fit woman, had finally found a List Man who was nuts about her. He was an accountant, very religious (like she is), and adored everything about her. After dating him for three weeks, she came out of her bliss bubble and started fixating on his extra few pounds and his un-hip wardrobe. The extra pounds didn't bother her that much, but she was concerned about what other people would think about his clothes. She took him shopping, and he was so touched by her attention that it inspired him to start an exercise regimen. Of course, he never turned into a runway model, but he did turn out one big mother diamond!

If the Shoe Fits, Wear It

Sometimes it's because a man is doing all the right things that you think something must be wrong with him. You tell yourself he couldn't be that great if he's so easy to have. You try and find something wrong with him: He is too bald, chunky, short, poorly dressed, boring, goofy, and so on. He may be none of these things (or he may be all of them), but you will desperately try to find something—anything—wrong with him.

Why? Because after years of being conditioned that love should be hard work, you will have a hard time abandoning the games and just letting somebody love you. Don't make this mistake—if you let a good man go, you will regret it.

Steve was a handsome, charming attorney. After spending seven years in New York dating many beautiful women, he moved back to his native Minnesota for a job opportunity. He seriously dated several interesting, great-looking women, but the day he saw Wendy at the health club he was smitten. He spent weeks getting his courage up to ask her out. He would go on and on about her to whoever would listen. Wendy went out with Steve, but she wasn't that interested. After all, Steve adored her, and she much preferred to pine over the guy who had dumped her recently.

She says, "I thought he was always really nice, and he was always available. It made me think that he didn't have any friends."

She also fixated on the ratty T-shirts he wore to the health club. In reality, Steve is very handsome and well dressed. But Wendy was so caught off-guard by this man who adored her that she used anything to discount him.

She finally realized that she had love under her nose. As she commented after they were engaged, "I don't know what I was thinking. He is the best man in the world." (PS: They've been married for five years and have a son, Jack.)

Open your heart up to love, and it will find you. In dating, we have all felt low and desperate, and sometimes we've felt overconfident and even arrogant. But you only need to aim at being your true "stripped-down" self to find the Fairy Tale. It's the *you* in your bedroom at night reading a book, or the *you* singing show tunes in the shower and planning your day. Or the *you* who daydreams that you are Elizabeth Bennet from *Pride and Prejudice*. It's the *you* perhaps nobody else truly knows. As women, we are so used to putting on our "game face." Being stripped down may make you feel vulnerable, codependent, and sometimes a bit off-kilter. These feelings will be replaced by pure joy when you meet your List Man and he falls in love with the real *you*.

Sometimes it can be really hard to allow a nice man to love you. It doesn't feel comfortable after spending months and years with men who wouldn't commit. As girls, we were conditioned to worship and chase the unobtainable "popular" guys in high school. You need only attend your ten- or twenty-year reunion to see that the "popular boys" are still living within a block of the old high school and playing on the Babe's Sports Bar softball team. If you yourself are hip and cool, then the person that you choose will be drenched in your stardust, so don't bother with those so-called popular boys anymore.

If you can't let a List Man be good to you, you may have self-esteem issues. Thank goodness that self-esteem *can* be bought! Not through extreme makeovers (although they can help, too) but through therapy. Therapy helps you get to know yourself. You will learn to recognize the great things you have going for you and how to become your own biggest fan. You will distance yourself from bad relationships and situations that make you feel insecure. With that foundation, it will be very easy for you to figure out what you want for your future and to decide on the type of man with whom you want to share your future (a List Man, no doubt).

There truly is a perfect fit for you—if you know what you are looking for. If you have confidence and you love yourself, you will be attractive to a man regardless of your perceived shortcomings. For every type of woman, there is a man who will love her as she is. Make it your goal to really define what makes a man a man. And then make it your mission in life never to love anybody who doesn't love you. The key thing to remember is that if a man has the good taste to approach you and ask you out, it says a lot about him.

Move Forward with Passion and Purpose

Everything you have ever done has brought you to this point. This is the path that will lead you to true love if you just keep moving forward with your head held high and your heart open. Try not to overthink the process. *The List* is easy because it is simple and universal. It doesn't matter if you are a Hollywood starlet or an average gal. These seven actions apply to everybody. *The List* isn't some big piece of modern art. It isn't up for interpretation or "yeah, buts." It is *The List,* and it is not to be debated or changed.

To make your journey easier, you're going to learn the stories of three women as you read through the book. Megan, Tara, and Christine are composites of several friends and acquaintances; many of these women are happily married now. All of these women did some serious soul-searching and decided to use *The List* to find love.

LIFE IN LISTOPIA

MEGAN

Megan is twenty-five years old. She met her now ex-boyfriend, Colin, at a bar soon after she graduated from college, and they dated for two years. Megan has always wanted to be married by age twenty-seven. She wants a big family and wants to get started on it by the time she's twenty-eight. And after she became exclusive with Colin, this seemed within reach. Everything started off so well! She figured that they would get engaged after a year of dating and be married a year after engagement. But no such luck. There were vacations and sub-par jewelry and promises whispered in the night. But three months, six months, a year, two years went by and still nothing.

Even though she knew deep inside that Colin was stalling, Megan couldn't bring herself to break up with him. She and Colin went to weddings together. They attended work events together. They spent holidays together. They shared all the same friends. Megan was scared to death to leave the relationship, and she was also embarrassed. Her friends and family members told her to "keep her options open," but she didn't want to admit that she was wrong. She didn't want to start over from scratch. "After all," she thought, "fifty percent of my dating lifespan is exhausted."

When she thought about this, frustration and fear would overtake her. That's when she would bring up marriage with Colin. Of course, Colin wasn't nearly as concerned about getting married. He felt that if all of the stars were aligned and he met the perfect woman, he might get married. But he knew plenty of men who had waited until they were forty for marriage. By that time, they had "done" the scene and were ready to have a family and settle down. He figured that if things didn't work out with Megan, he still had a good ten years left to find a wife.

Colin was very attracted to Megan and liked the stability of the relationship, so when Megan issued ultimatums, Colin assured her that he was happy with her and wanted "to get married someday." He didn't want to chance losing Megan because he thought she *might* be the right one—he just wasn't sure. When she kept the pressure on, Colin put the decision on her. He told her if she couldn't deal with where he was, then they probably needed to break up. He knew that he would miss her companionship but didn't want to be rushed into marriage.

Megan recognized The Stall. She didn't want to be placated anymore. She wanted to be married! She asked herself a key question: "If a wonderful man came into your life right now and swept you off your feet, would you leave Colin?" Her initial answer was "No." But then she asked herself a follow-up question: "Why are you intent on marrying somebody who isn't excited about marrying you?"

And finally she got it. Right then and there she decided that she was ready to clean her slate. She was twenty-five and wanted to get married by the time she was twenty-seven. Could it still happen? She initially had a hard time buying into the idea. She had always believed it would take at least a couple of years of dating before a man would propose. After reading *The List,* she realized that two years with Colin was more than enough time to realize that he wouldn't be offering a proposal. She thought, "He may not realize that he's not going to marry me, but I realize it." She got up her nerve and dumped him. He begged for a little more time, even asked her to move in with him, but she stood her ground. It was tough. She cried a thousand tears. But after a couple of months of mourning she is ready to get back out there again. Enough time has been wasted!

TARA

Tara is thirty years old. She has always wanted a husband and family. During college, she dated a man for three years and thought that he was "the one." He kept her on a string and dumped her after graduation. At that point, she decided that she wanted to be married by age twenty-six—at the latest. But her actions didn't match her words. She spent years ignoring the nice guys and kept wasting time on inaccessible men. With every month and year that passed, Tara started feeling more anxious. She was so impatient for the right man to come along that she would get her hopes up too quickly. Every time a man asked her out, she was so consumed with the possibilities that lay ahead she barely noticed if he even liked her. She is at the point now where she is willing to invest her time in any man who is halfway interested in her. She figures that she can "work" with him and make him love her. She has forgotten what she wants from a mate and marriage. At this point, just about any warm body will do.

She's not picky and will date just about anybody who takes the initiative to approach her (as long as he's good-looking, that is). They all show interest in the beginning, but after a date or two, things fizzle. They can probably sense that Tara gets too serious too fast. They say things like, "I love my nieces" and throw out enticing lines like, "I'm ready to settle down" that make her think that she is the one. Then they go on their way.

One of the men she dated, Mike, came on very strong initially. They went out a few times and then things slowed down. She still calls Mike and he is always happy to hear from her. They still get together from time to time. They have a great time together, and Mike tells her how much fun he has with her (usually after a drink or two). Mike really liked Tara in the beginning, but after a few weeks of hanging out, he just sort of lost the urge to pursue her. He doesn't really know why. He doesn't think he is leading Tara on. She knows that they aren't serious. He figures that if she didn't want to see him, she wouldn't call. He really has his eye on another girl, but it is taking longer to get her attention than he thought it would. When he is bored or frustrated, he calls Tara. She is always up for a good time.

Most of Tara's relationships last from a few weeks to a few months. She gets so upset when things don't work out that she needs to "recover" between relationships and pull herself together to face the dating world again. Her cell phone is full of the numbers of guys she can count on to call her up every now and then, and she'll usually accept dates from them. It's better than being alone on the weekends, she figures. During "recovery" periods, she pours her energy into her career and friendships with other single women. Sometimes, she can convince herself that she doesn't want to get married at all.

Tara liked what *The List* had to say, but it seemed far-fetched. Could she really cut her losses early in the game? She asked herself a key question: "If a great-looking, successful, funny, interesting guy waits a week to ask you out after your first date, do you go out with him again?" She hedged. Were there really men out there who would do the things described in *The List*? She then asked herself, "Why do you have such a low opinion of yourself to make time for someone who doesn't make it a priority to make time for you?"

She decided that she was done with her method of dating. She wanted new results. In the past, she had accepted any and all dates that came her way in hopes that quantity would bring quality. That approach hadn't worked. Besides, while she was wasting time on the wrong men, she wasn't really available for a List Man.

Tara has realistically reset her clock. At thirty, she figures she'll give herself two more years to find a mate and get married. The first order of business is to figuratively dump her menagerie of commitment-phobic men by deleting every single number from her cell phone with the exception of her mother, sister, hair stylist, and dentist. After reading *The List*, she will no longer take calls from the time-wasting men of her past.

CHRISTINE

Christine is thirty-nine years old. She is a successful attorney who makes more money than most of the men she dates. She's confident and strong, but she's also lonely. She's tired of taking vacations alone or with her few remaining single girlfriends. She's grown wary of all the business happy hours and dinner meetings at fancy restaurants and would love nothing more than to come home from the office to watch television and eat pizza with her soul mate.

She dates occasionally but really doesn't have time to actively seek out men or stay in a long-term relationship that won't go anywhere. The men she dates are always fellow professionals she meets through friends or work colleagues. They are usually her age, in her tax bracket, and in some cases have been married before. They like her "take-charge" attitude and view her as someone who's confident enough in her own life not to need marriage.

She's lucky to date two or three different men over the course of a year and believes her lack of dating action is due to her income and age. Why should a woman of her qualities waste time actively pursuing the dating scene? She tells herself that she's too old for games, and since she won't settle, she may just need to be happy by herself. As for the few men who do come into her life, she typically dates them for a month or two before they break up in some lackluster manner.

One of her relationships lasted six months. Ken, age forty-five, seemed to have great promise. Christine met Ken through a professional organization. Even though he was divorced with two teenagers, Christine really fell for him. They became an instant couple. She felt like a teenager with him, and he loved her energy and passion for life. She was the complete opposite of his college sweetheart and ex-wife, who was a homemaker. Christine started mentioning the long-term within a few months. Ken really liked her and would have been happy to be exclusive indefinitely. But Christine wanted marriage. She figured he would come around. After a nasty divorce, he wasn't interested in getting married again anytime soon. And kids were out of the question. He broke it off with Christine and is seeing another woman. He was happily surprised to find out that after twenty years "off the market," he was still a hot commodity.

Christine doesn't want to invest any more time or energy in the wrong men. Although she hates to admit it, loneliness is taking an emotional toll, little by little.

After reading the first part of *The List*, Christine completed her "Must Haves/Nice to Haves" list and realized that she has really been dating the same man over and over again. And none of these men really shared her values. She asked herself, "Why do I think I am so much better than some of the nice guys who have been interested in me in the past?"

She has no answer. At thirty-nine, Christine realizes that she can no longer waste time picking some men apart while rationalizing the bad behavior of others. She knows she doesn't have a moment to lose. She has always been assertive in the workplace, so why not make an aggressive goal of being married by her forty-first birthday? Dreams of a big white dress may have never been foremost in her mind, but lately, she has had to admit that she does like to occasionally indulge in the fantasy of a fabulous sheath dress and an intimate wedding on Martha's Vineyard. And then maybe—just maybe—she could still have a child.

WRAP-UP

You bought this book to star in your own Fairy Tale. To do this, you need to believe that there is somebody in the world who will love you as you are. You won't have to do anything but "be." And what can be more fulfilling than that?

After reading *The List,* you will begin to see the light at the end of the tunnel. As you go down your new path toward the bright light of true love, keep these last tips in mind:

☑ *Don't expect to find a great man if you haven't done the work necessary to be your best.* Whether it's going to therapy, confiding in a happily married friend, attending religious services, meditating, exercising, embracing nature, or writing in a journal, do activities that will help you "get deep" so you can focus on who you are and what you want for the future. Become your own best friend. With a strong core in place, you will feel secure and you will be ready to find love.

☑ *Don't wait around to become the victim of a breakup.* If you do, you will not only lose the time wasted on the wrong man, you will lose your self-confidence.

☑ *Don't waste time regretting the past.* It is water under the bridge. Learn from past mistakes and accept them as a vital part of your unique path. Adjust your goals as necessary, and use your time wisely.

☑ *Don't get frustrated.* Everyone can sense frustration; men often confuse it with desperation. Have faith in the future. Believe that your future is bright and that your dreams can and will come true.

☑ *Do date strategically.* Take your woman math into account. Date as many men as you can, and use *The List* to judge them as quickly as possible.

☑ *Do walk away if you have issued any type of ultimatum to a current boyfriend.* It is already too late if you've had to say "or else."

☑ *Do build your self-confidence by dumping men who don't do the things on* The List. Refusing to settle builds your self-confidence, and men love self-confident women.

☑ *Don't second-guess yourself.* Go with your gut. If you feel like you are "working" to make a man like you, it is too late. Follow *The List*, and everything will work out the way it is meant to work out.

And, most important:

☑ *Take the vow:* I will only spend time with a man who does everything on The List.

THREE

List

Item 1:

HE MAKES
THE FIRST MOVE

The first item to check off on *The List* seems obvious. When a man wants to be with you, he knows it right away. You should know it right away, too, because he will approach you. You won't have to do much at all. He will see you and know that he wants to talk to you. He will be immediately attracted to you and will want to find out if your personality is as becoming as your physical appearance.

It is not going out on limb here to say that with very few exceptions, if you approach a man first, you will not marry him. Let's bring this back to high school simplicity. Who hasn't had a massive crush on the unattainable cute boy? You'd fantasize about Johnny Quarterback and write his last name next to your first name on your Trapper Keeper. But he never knew you existed. Or, if he did, he probably thought you were really weird for stalking him. This kind of puppy love is harmless and pretty common at sixteen, but it's totally pathetic at age twenty-six. Nothing has changed! No matter how great you are, "going after" a man is a waste of time, and *The List* is about maximizing your time. Although you can't control whom you're attracted to, you also can't control who will be attracted to you. You lose when you go after a man because *The List* is about what *he* will do to win your heart—not what you will do to make him notice you.

Your List Man Will Find You

Most happily married women didn't even notice that their husbands were looking at them.

Editor and writer Gail was a young widow, only twenty-seven, when she met Larry. After six months of marriage, her husband had died of a heart attack. She was grieving beyond belief, but that didn't stop a List Man from finding her. Two months after the funeral, Gail's friends dragged her to a mellow gathering to get her out of her house. Larry, a musician with long hair falling halfway down his back, spotted the six-foot-tall squeaky-clean blond beauty across the room. Although he knew of her tragic circumstance, he was immediately smitten. Larry had every reason not to approach Gail, but he couldn't help himself. He took his time, was careful not to scare her, and then still made his move.

The last thing on Gail's mind that night was meeting her future second husband. As many women are, Gail was in her own world when she met Larry.

Larry struck up a conversation with her and they talked for hours. Gail felt comfortable pouring her heart out to him. She never felt like she would turn him off by pretending to be in a place where she wasn't. Besides, she wasn't even thinking about courtship. It just found her. When Gail decided that she was ready to start dating some months later, Larry was patiently waiting for her. He completed all the items on *The List*. (PS: Larry and Gail have been married for nine years and the proud parents of Abby and Grace.)

Jane, a graphics designer, met Mike, an artist, when she was twenty-five and he was thirty-two. She attended a party with her boyfriend at the time, who introduced her to Mike. "By the end of the evening, my boyfriend heard Mike ask me to lunch and jokingly asked if I wanted him to step into the next room," Jane shares.

The first date led to instant and constant togetherness:

"Right away, Mike and I both had birthdays and were together for those. On my birthday my siblings had a surprise party for me. I was

on to them but played dumb. The set-up was that my brother and his wife told me that we were going out to dinner and I should bring a date. They assumed it would be the guy they knew I was dating. Imagine their surprise when I walked in with Mike and not my boyfriend! Mike was more surprised than anyone. Straightaway he was thrown into a room with everybody I knew."

A few weeks after their first meeting in August, Mike mentioned he was interested in the "long haul." They were engaged in October. Jane's friends were concerned about how fast the relationship was moving and had an "intervention" to tell her that she didn't need to go through with her wedding. Mike and Jane were married at the end of December. (PS: They've been married for twenty years and have two grown sons, Alex and Joe.)

Sid (introduced in Chapter 1) met his wife, Tricia, at a restaurant party that his friend invited him to:

"Even though I almost didn't go, I actually thought, 'What the heck, I might meet someone.' I was talking to a few friends when I saw this really beautiful girl walk in. I thought, 'I wish she was in our group.' She walked toward the back of the restaurant and I went on talking to my friends and tried to catch her eye. A few minutes later, she came back to the front where we were seated. I smiled at her and she took the seat next to me. From that point we talked the rest of the night and had a really great conversation. I overheard that another guy had asked her for her phone number. That only increased my courage. I asked her out on the spot."

Norm met his future wife Deborah on the job, and he remembers the moment well:

"A salesperson at the company motioned me over to his desk to check out a picture of the new girl on the company intranet. In Deborah's candid company picture, she had the expression of a deer caught in the beam of headlights. But she was adorable. Her hair reminded me of one of Charlie Brown's schoolmates, the one with the naturally curly hair. Deb wore a dark brown blouse with a scarf tied around her neck. She must have made an impression because I haven't seen the picture in nearly five years and I can recall it vividly. I knew I had to approach her right away."

Remember The Alarm? The Alarm is why if a man likes you, he will approach you immediately. It is futile to try to convince yourself that a man is a List Man if he never even made a clear first move. You may try to pursue or be "friends" with a good-looking man who isn't interested in you romantically. You tell yourself that if the man gets to know your great personality, he will grow to love you. Or if you can provide emotional support to him during a hard time, he will grow to love you. You may dismiss people who tell you not to pursue men. You think these naysayers are "old fashioned." Old fashioned—maybe. Married—probably.

Here's what our panel of men said about how you can tell if a man wants you:

1. He will approach you. If he is at a party or a bar, it will be easy. If he sees you in a public place (like a grocery store or

bookstore), he will find a way to be in close proximity to you. He will try to strike up a conversation. Or, if he is too shy or doesn't have time to gather his thoughts (because he is so stricken by your beauty), he will go back to the same place, at the same time, for at least a week in the hopes of seeing you again. And believe this: If he gets a second chance—he will not blow it!

2. He may be a bit uncomfortable around you. Or, as one man confided, "He will try very hard to act comfortable around you." He realizes that he likes you and is afraid that you may not like him back—that makes him uncomfortable. But he realizes that if he acts strangely, you may be turned off. So he really has to go out of his way to seem at ease.

3. He will try to force some opening for conversation. If you are at a dinner party with friends in common or at a singles gathering, this will be easy to do. If you are strangers in public, he will do something very subtle (to you) but obvious (to him), such as walking past or toward you and saying, "Excuse me" within earshot. Hopefully, you will pick up on this and smile at him if he catches your eye. But that is all you will need to do.

"The Moment"

Men, like women, understand that romance is a rare commodity. Just because he doesn't watch Nora Ephron movies, or talk about his dreams, or buy magazines featuring Jennifer Aniston or Jude Law on the cover doesn't mean that he doesn't know a romantic opportunity when he sees it. Even if a man pretends that romance is a "chick" thing, he quickly understands that if he lets the moment pass, it may not come again for a long time.

He isn't the only one who understands that an important moment is about to happen. In his mind, other people will see him approach you. He feels as though everything freezes as he makes his move and that all eyes are on him. This is why he is scared and uncomfortable. Nothing could be worse than his rejection. That's why a woman looking for love must pick up on a man's cues and be as open-minded and pleasant as possible when a List Man makes his move.

Even if you immediately think that he isn't "good enough" for you, remember the risk he is taking by approaching you in the first place. Also, don't forget that a List Man is a rare and special man who can't be judged before you've given him a chance. Let him into your life, and see how he does against *The List.* If somebody better comes along who does well against *The List*, you can say your goodbyes then.

While you can't judge a book by its cover, you can judge it readily by its content. In the spirit of weeding out losers as quickly as possible, it is important to pay attention to his behavior during this important moment. Even though he is under an incredible amount of pressure, he should be a gentleman. He shouldn't try to manipulate too much of your time, or spend time bragging about himself and being obnoxious. He shouldn't be paying attention to your girlfriends or to his own friends during this moment. This is *your* moment. He should ask you some polite questions about you or make pleasant conversation about whatever is happening around you.

He is a man on a mission, and that mission is to get a date with you. After his initial approach, he knows two things:

1. He is attracted to you.
2. You are receptive to him.

He can figure out how the chemistry plays out during a date. He may ask you out on the spot, or he may ask for your phone number. If he asks you out on the spot, go for it—you'll be doing so well that you can not only check *The List* Item 1, but Item 2 as well! If he is going to marry you, you don't need to play hard to get.

If You Make Excuses for Him, He's Not a List Man

For many women, it seems that "When it rains, it pours." They either have too many men or none at all. Sometimes, even if you are being open-minded and approachable and doing what you need to do, you will hit a dry spell. Don't be tempted to second-guess *The List* and start approaching men. You can be at your very best and be the cutest girl in the room, and sometimes it still doesn't matter. You can't control chemistry—it just is. If a man doesn't approach you, you haven't sounded The Alarm and there is absolutely nothing to be done about it. You may be a gorgeous blond, but that won't matter if he likes brunettes. You may be a scant size six but that won't matter if he likes curves. You may have a great cosmopolitan job, but that doesn't matter if he likes schoolteacher types.

Take, for instance, George W. Bush. Even though he pretends to be a lowly cowboy from Texas, it's no secret that he is a rich, pedigreed, Ivy

League blue blood. In his day, can you imagine all the Texas beauties who must have thrown themselves at him? But who sounded The Alarm—a buff, blond beauty queen? No. A pretty, soft-spoken librarian got him to the altar in three months. And all these years later, it is clear to see that he is still absolutely, positively in love with her.

There is nothing that you can do to *make* a man be attracted to you. This is not to say that you should walk around in sweatpants without makeup. To the contrary, you should always look your best because then you will feel your best. When you feel your best, you exude confidence, and men are drawn to confidence. But make no mistake: If a man likes you, he won't really care if you are wearing a $250 dress or notice if your roots are showing. He won't care if you think you are thirty pounds overweight. For whatever reason, when you have sounded The Alarm, he is drawn to you.

For all of these reasons, it is best for a man to approach a woman with whom he is smitten. Do these excuses for why a man isn't coming up to you sound familiar?

> ▷ "He's just shy."
> ▷ "He thinks I have a boyfriend."
> ▷ "He thinks his friend likes me."
> ▷ "I caught him looking at me so he must like me."
> ▷ "He's intimidated because I'm with a group of friends."
> ▷ "He can't think of what to say."

There are countless stories of how men have overcome all the odds and approached the woman that they eventually married. Don't waste time making excuses.

Are There Exceptions to This List Item?

Sure, there are happily married women who have made the first move. But these are rare exceptions. In all cases, these women were very happy with their single status and didn't need *The List* to help them out. All of them also told us that, in retrospect, they saw that if they had a little more patience, the men would have asked them out.

Caroline, a professional counselor, met and married Justin, a List Man:

"The women I know who ask men out are often anxious to find wholeness in a relationship instead of within themselves. By making the first move, they open themselves up to profound rejection and are more likely to settle. The chasing part of courtship is such a dignity killer!"

The List isn't about explaining and rationalizing exceptions. *The List* isn't about the actions *you* take. *The List* is about identifying the actions *he* will make during courtship. Ashley, introduced in the introduction, puts it perfectly:

"Don't waste your time and emotion trying to make things happen. You may wiggle a little attention out of him, but it's one-sided and not true courtship. You may even get him to marry you, but do you want to be with a man you're always going to have to "light a fire under" to make him show some interest in you? Make the effort to be happy as a single person. Take time to figure out what makes you happy and sad, inspired and depressed. Figure out your goals

that are not contingent on getting married. Learn that you are an individual with strengths and weaknesses, beauty and flaws, but altogether unique and special. Be realistic about the men you set your heart on, but don't settle."

Think about it this way. In the world of dating, we all have a proper role to play. If we deviate from that role, we are upsetting the natural course of things. If you push something that is not meant to happen, you are not available to meet a List Man. At the same time, you are keeping him from meeting a woman who sounds The Alarm.

If you think of courtship in this manner, you will become more self-assured, and men will sense this. You will be a welcome breath of fresh air compared to all the desperate women who spend their time and energy trying to control something they can't (what men think) and not enough time controlling something they can (their own outlooks).

LIFE IN LISTOPIA

MEGAN

Megan has embraced her newfound single status, and she is happy to discover that she is young and cute enough to be approached by a lot of men out on "the scene." Initially she only goes out with groups of girlfriends, and most men approach all of them together with groups of their friends. She watches as one of her more aggressive girlfriends goes out of her way to give a certain man special attention and to offer her phone number. Megan resists the urge to do the same. She decides to follow *The List* and to let the man make the first move. It is hard, though! Sometimes it seems like her friends who make the first move have a lot more dates than she does.

After a couple of months of this, she quickly realizes that these are not List Men. She makes an effort to go out on her own. She joins a singles group at her church and a college alumni group, and she starts volunteering a few hours a week for a local political campaign. After about a month of going to different functions, she starts to meet all sorts of new and interesting people, but she feels a little sad that no dating prospects have yet approached her. Almost six months have passed since she left Colin, and now she is really starting to worry that she has made a mistake.

Then, at a casual barbecue with the college alumni group, Peter approaches her. He has come along with a friend and as soon as he sees Megan, he is smitten. He tries all night to move into the group of people she's talking to. She has obviously made a lot of friends, and he only knows the buddy he came with. Finally, when some people start to leave the party, Peter makes a beeline to Megan. Megan smiles. She thinks that he seems nice, but kind of dorky with his John Lennon glasses and severe lack of sun exposure.

Peter politely introduces himself and asks how long she has attended these get-togethers. Then he asks if she will be going to any others in the future. After a few more minutes of polite conversation, Megan excuses herself to go out with a few girls to a nearby bar. She thinks, "Maybe I'll have better luck there. Peter is nice, but he isn't my type and he hasn't asked for my phone number."

At the bar, she finds herself checking out a really great-looking guy. Finally, he looks her way and smiles at her. But the bar is crowded and he looks like he is in deep discussion with a business colleague. An hour later—just as she is settling the tab with her friends—he makes his way across to her. He asks if he can buy her a drink. She replies, "No, I'm actually on my way out." He tries to make conversation with her, but she is flustered. It would have been so much easier if he approached her an hour ago! Now she has other people breathing down her neck waiting to take her table.

They talk briefly. She learns his name is Drew and that he is in sales and works in the same building that she does. As she starts walking toward the door, he gives her his business card and says he would love to have lunch sometime.

So, after a long dry spell, it's raining men for Megan!

TARA

Once Tara makes the decision to do things differently, she feels incredibly positive. She immediately lets her close friends and family know that she is starting a new chapter. She will only date serious men who do the things on *The List*. She decides she needs to meet higher-quality men and signs up for one of the values-driven online dating services. In addition, she also hosts monthly "matchmaker" dinner parties. She even puts her creative skills to use by designing a cute invitation, like this:

ುೢಕಿಃ೩

It's a Matchmaker Party
For you and your mate,
Bring a bachelor along
For Tara to date

Party starts at 7:30 P.M.
Don't be late!

p.s. Shhh—remember not to tell
him what's going on!

Tara starts by asking her happily married friends to her party. At the start of each party, she asks each couple to tell how they met. She asks them all to keep her in mind if they think of any great single men who are interested in marriage and whom they think will be right for her. At her second party, she invites some happily married "friends of friends" and even an older coworker and his wife to her party. She is such a delightful hostess that the couples all fall in love with her and put her at the top of their list.

Sometimes she feels embarrassed; sometimes she feels like Bridget Jones, but she can't argue with the results. After careful scrutiny, she meets nearly a dozen men online and is set up on a several dates resulting from the dinner parties. Most of the men seem nice enough, but when it comes to *The List*, they fizzle quickly.

But all is not lost. One of the women who attended Tara's party (a coworker's wife) gives Tara's phone number to Bret. Tara is told that he is very funny and good-looking. And he is very excited to meet Tara. Of course Tara can't resist Googling him on the Internet. A few clicks later, she has his picture and bio from the architecture firm where he works. A few weeks have passed since the dinner party, so she makes up an excuse to call her coworker's wife and coyly brings Bret up. "Oh, honey, he's going to call you but I think he was going to China sometime this month on business. I told him what a doll you are and he can hardly wait to meet you." Tara feels great about that and allows herself to fantasize about a man she hasn't met yet.

The next day, a man named Patrick comes through on her online match list. Within twenty-four hours of the match, he e-mails her saying that he thinks she is very pretty and likes her profile, and that he would like to meet her. She gives him her phone number on the next e-mail and he calls the next day.

Unlike any of the other men she has met over this service, Patrick seems downright aggressive. She's a little unsure, but remembers what *The List* says and she can definitely qualify him as making the first move. She's not sure what to think at this point. And guess who else makes his initial approach? Bret has finally found his phone. When it rains, it pours.

CHRISTINE

Christine tackles her dating situation with the same tenacity she tackles her work projects. She is going to be strategic and quickly assess her strengths and weaknesses. In addition to *The List*, she stocks up on any dating book she can find that will help her with her mission.

After looking hard at her lack of success over the past twenty years of dating, she sees common denominators among the men she has dated. So she decides to take six-figure incomes and Burberry suits off her list of "Must Haves" and goes out looking for something completely different. She quits all the professional organizations she belonged to and even forces herself to leave the office by five so she can meet friends for dinner or just hang out at Starbucks to enjoy people-watching and the latest issue of *Vogue*. She weans herself from her weekly Saturday spa days and starts spending time at Home Depot. She embarks upon home fix-up projects and even joins her neighborhood association. She sees a lot of cute guys, but she also notices a lot of gold rings.

Christine is old enough and wise enough not to worry as she keeps moving toward her goal. Besides, she is really enjoying mastering new things, seeing new scenes, and meeting new people. After a few months she's been on four dates—more than she's been on in the last year. But none of the men make it far on *The List*. She decides to join the military-history book club at the local bookstore. (This isn't contrived—her dad was a navy pilot, and she's always been interested in the subject, but she's also savvy enough to know that the man-to-woman ratio may work in her favor.) Sure enough, at the very first meeting she meets Barry.

After going around in the circle, she learns that Barry is a telephone repairman who plays city-league hockey in his spare time. Christine introduces herself as an attorney who grew up with season tickets to the local NHL team. He approaches her right after the meeting and asks her to share a cup of coffee at the in-store coffee shop. She fights her urge to play hard-to-get and accepts happily.

She learns that Barry is divorced (he was married very young and the marriage only lasted a year) and has had several jobs in his life but that he likes his current company because of the stability and the benefits. He is only thirty-three years old. She does not learn how much money he's made in the market, what his "dreams" are, or where he vacationed last winter. She's a little nervous about his age, his income, and his seemingly happy-go-lucky nature—but he certainly did approach her, so she'll keep an open mind. Besides, he told her within the first five minutes of meeting her that he loved her red hair. She can't help but smile at that.

At work, one of Christine's recently divorced coworkers, Bill, has noticed her new routine and attitude. Christine has always had a crush on Bill and even considered asking him out but resisted the temptation. They have been on several business trips together and shared many dinners and conversations. But he has never asked her out . . . until now.

WRAP-UP

The List describes what actions a man will take if he is going to marry you. If you make the first move, you're making it impossible to measure his actions from the start. Patience is the most important attribute to possess during this stage.

Some women have a hard time accepting that when it comes to the initial stages of dating, they have no control over the process. They can't control whether a man will approach them, so they make the mistake of making the first move. Don't burn up your precious time and energy trying to work up the courage to approach a man. Be confident, and believe in what is meant to be. When you are conquering List Item 1, keep these points in mind:

- ☑ No matter how much you like him, you have to understand that the first move is his.

- ☑ Men who see you and think "Well, she's cute—maybe I should talk to her," but don't make the initial approach should be forgotten.

- ☑ If a man doesn't adore you, he doesn't deserve you.

- ☑ When a man approaches you, give him a chance. It takes a lot of guts to approach a woman like you.

☑ When a List Man comes your way, you don't have to play games or act a certain way. Be encouraging!

☑ If you are in a situation where you expect to be approached but aren't, don't worry about it. Be thankful that you aren't getting your hopes up over nothing.

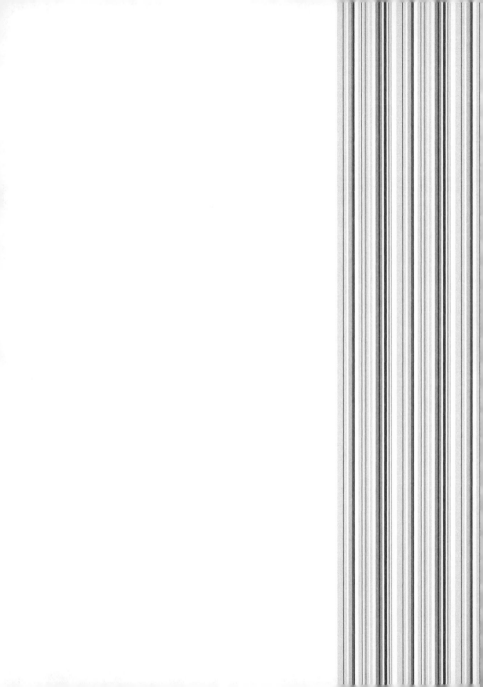

FOUR

List

Item 2:

HE CALLS YOU WITHIN
TWENTY-FOUR TO
FORTY-EIGHT HOURS
TO SET UP A FIRST DATE

Sometimes you can be so encouraged by a man's interest that you overlook the importance of a timely phone call. In the earliest stages of courtship, words don't count. Feelings don't count. Daydreams don't count. *Actions* count. That's why he needs to call you as soon as he possibly can.

Calling ASAP and making a date to see you is a measurable action, and it is the second sign that a man is a List Man. There is no other acceptable way (short of asking you out on the spot—which is the best method of all) to communicate the beginning of a promising relationship.

Why Is ASAP So Important?

First off, drill this into your head: If he is really excited about getting a date with you, he should and will call within twenty-four hours. If he calls within forty-eight hours, that is okay—but not as great as if he had called earlier. The only reason for this extra day's allowance is to cut some slack to those men who have been conditioned into thinking that if they call too soon, they will turn the woman off. But really, if he doesn't call you within twenty-four hours, don't get your hopes up too high.

Whether you have met him at a friend's wedding, on the bus to work, or online, he needs to make that phone call within twenty-four hours to prove that he is really interested and not just bored. Even if he is going out of town on business, or lives in another part of the country altogether—the List Man will still call you right away.

If forty-eight hours pass and you haven't heard from him, just forget he exists. Every man worth having knows about the two-day rule. If he wants you enough, he will set his ego aside and call you within this time frame because it is all about making you happy.

Men who don't call right away have a reason, and the reason is never good. Remember, many men interviewed for this book weren't List Men in the eyes of the women they *didn't* marry. They said that if they didn't call a woman right away it was because they were either seeing another woman or they were simply bored and wanted somebody to talk to. A timely phone call is an early and sure indicator of interest.

Even if a man isn't in the habit of calling women so quickly after meeting them, he will call you quickly if you have sounded The Alarm. He has never felt this way before, so all of the rules about playing it cool that he used in the past—or that his friends encourage him to use now—are out the window. He has already risked life and limb approaching you—why would he go to all that trouble just to sit on his hands for a week? He will call you as soon as possible for these reasons:

1. He wants to talk to you so he can set up a date.
2. He doesn't want to take a chance that you'll change your mind about him or forget about him altogether.
3. Seeing you is the single most important thing in his life at the moment.

Sorry, but e-mail doesn't count. E-mail is for business purposes or to keep in touch with friends and family members. As it relates to courtship, it is lazy, impersonal, and too convenient. Initially, there is no reason for a man to even have your e-mail address. A List Man won't ask for it. If a man somehow figures out your e-mail address and sends you a message, politely respond, "Hey! I really shouldn't receive personal e-mails at work. Sorry. Talk to you soon." He will get the hint. He will understand that he should call you (he should want to!), and you will not spend time at work waiting for his e-mails. You haven't seen him in action enough to know if he is even worth thinking about. During the first few weeks of dating, stay away from e-mail.

Let him take the lead once he has made the call, but try to make it easy on him. This is a scary junior-high flashback for him. When he initially approached you, he was on an adrenaline high. (He may have even had a couple of drinks in him.) He knows that you may have decided he isn't good enough for you. An enthusiastic, "Hey it's great to hear from you," or, "I was hoping you would call" will give him the confidence to move forward with his agenda.

If He Doesn't Call ASAP, Don't Make Excuses for Him

Because action is the only thing you can measure at this point, excuses aren't going to cut it. If he is a List Man, he will jump through fire to get to you. He will cross the desert for you. Excuses like these are a waste of time:

- ▷   "He doesn't want to seem too anxious."
- ▷   "He must be really busy."
- ▷   "He said that he would be out of town."
- ▷   "He must have misplaced my number."
- ▷   "Maybe he thought I wasn't interested."

If a man waits a few weeks or even a month before calling, how excited can he truly be about you? Not very. The only way you should even consider going on a first date with a person who delays his first phone call is if he takes accountability immediately and offers a reason. Still, don't get your hopes up.

Here are the *only* acceptable reasons for his not calling ASAP:

1. You have a mutual friend, and he is feeling out your status and your receptiveness to an approach. But the forty-eight-hour rule still applies. If he hasn't contacted you within forty-eight hours after approaching you, he had better have contacted your mutual acquaintance. After that, he needs to call you right away.
2. He is severely injured (preferably in a coma) or is, unfortunately, dead. (And if he doesn't call ASAP, he may as well be.)

If he calls after your deadline has passed, just tell him you have other plans. If he is relentless in his pursuit, you can give him one more chance if you are totally bored, but proceed with caution. Tell him the truth:

"You know, _____, I'm used to guys calling me right away to ask me on dates. I only go out with guys who are really excited about seeing me. And if a guy doesn't call within a couple of days, it's usually a pretty good sign that he isn't."

Then just wait for a response. What you need to hear at this point is complete contrition for his failure to call. He needs to say that he screwed up or that he was afraid you would think he was too anxious. If he tries to make you feel stupid in any way or if he says that four days, or a week, or a month isn't waiting a long time— blow him off. He won't marry you, so you are losing nothing. Just say:

> *"I'm really sorry. You have your own way of doing things, and I have my way. And I only go out with guys who call me quickly. You can think whatever you want to, but that's just how I am. Let's just leave it at that. Goodbye."*

You will feel *so* good about yourself. And you will not waste weeks, months, or years on a non–List Man. Remind yourself that because he wasn't compelled to see you right away, he won't ever be that passionate about you.

He Won't Merely **Try** to Reach You—He **Will** Reach You

Now that you have established exactly when he will call you, you need to add one more essential requirement to the mix: He will not only call you, he will *reach* you.

Since a List Man's goal is to ask you on a date, the talking is only a means to that end. Therefore, he will be sure to contact you when he is most likely to reach you. It is much better for a man to wait to call and reach you at 7:00 P.M. (when it is likely that you will be home and available to talk to him), than at noon (when you are obviously at work) and leave a message on your machine. You can tell yourself, "Wow, he liked me so much that he called me at noon! He couldn't even wait until the evening!" But he called you at a time when you couldn't be reached, so it doesn't even count.

Worse yet, you are put in a terrible position when he leaves a message. You have two equally icky options: (1) Call him back, which really isn't an option; or (2) Wait by the phone until he calls you, which, based on his past performance, could be at any hour of the day or night. If a man is a habitual message-leaver and never seems to actually reach you, it is because reaching you isn't a priority. For whatever reason, he is stalling or trying to string things along. He definitely isn't in a hurry to see you because to see you and get a date, he needs to talk to you. He may have time to waste, but you don't.

You know how it is at work when you have an uncomfortable phone call to make—perhaps to inform a customer that the shipment will be three weeks late or to tell a colleague that his project is completely botched? You hope and pray that you will get the person's voice mail. It's the same thing with these guys. They don't actually want to talk to you—they just want to check you off their list. But now, it's about your *List*.

Not only will the List Man's phone call come when you are home, but it will be at a respectful time as well. On school nights, he will call you between 7:00 and 9:30 P.M. An early phone call means too many unknowns that may make you unavailable. You could still be at work, or at the gym, or eating dinner, or walking your dog, or you may simply be unwinding from a long day at work. And he won't call you too late because it is inappropriate for somebody you don't know to call you after 9:30 P.M. at night. You may be taking a bath, doing your nails, or getting ready for bed.

If his deadline falls during a weekend, he will call you in the late morning or early afternoon. He will assume that you are out at night. If he calls you during the day and slyly figures out that you are available that very night, he may ask you out on the spot. If you are free, go out with him.

Either way, the List Man will call you at a time when he can focus on you. Hopefully, he will call you from his home and not from his cell phone. But that's just an annoyance, not a deal breaker.

Yes, You Can Wait by the Phone

And now for something unexpected: You get to sit your hopeful little self by the phone. Waiting by the phone is a bad idea when you don't know if it is going to ring. We've all spent months (years, even) waiting by the phone for a guy to call. It is usually a total waste of time. But since *The List* requires that he call within twenty-four to forty-eight hours after approaching you, and you have pinpointed the time when he will call, you can break from the old adage "Don't wait by the phone." If you've just met a man who saw you and wanted you and was man enough to get your phone number, you are allowed to sit by the phone and wait for his call until the forty-eight-hour deadline has passed. You'll only be waiting for a few hours on a couple of evenings.

Playing hard-to-get at this point is just a stupid strategy. You are already his "dream girl" at this early stage. This is not the time to play games and be unavailable. If a man calls within twenty-four to forty-eight hours of meeting you, reward him by letting him hear your voice. He'll think that you are interested, which is important positive reinforcement. As long as he is a List Man, waiting by the phone for a small window of time won't be too torturous for you because he will call.

If he isn't a List Man, he won't call for a few days or a week, but you won't be waiting by the phone. By then, you will have already figured out that he is wasting your time.

A List Man Schedules a Date ASAP

Seeing you as soon as possible is a List Man's number-one priority. That's why he will "close the deal" by asking you out during that first phone conversation. Be aware that a List Man may be shy or unsure if you are receptive to him. When you pick up the phone, give him a big, friendly, "Hi! I'm glad you called." But then let him do most of the talking. Try to steer away from becoming phone friends.

An interested man will ask you out on a date and schedule that date to take place within a few days. He may have something planned, such as catching a movie or grabbing a cup of coffee. If he asks you out immediately, by all means, go! If he called you quickly, there is no harm in seeing him right away. List Men do not enjoy playing mind games. Why would they? Their mind is already made up.

Don't pretend you're busy if you aren't. He's worthy of clearing your calendar because he's done all the right things so far. The List Man will not think you are desperate; he will be delighted he can see you so soon. If you have a full calendar that can't be cleared, make sure you let him know that you really do want to see him. That way, he will not be deterred, and he will find a way to make it work. If you can't meet him for coffee tomorrow, then he should ask you for lunch the next day. If you have a meeting that day, then he should ask you for drinks the following day, and so on. A List Man in pursuit of his woman cannot be deterred—not by his schedule or yours—and he will get on your calendar ASAP.

When it comes to the first date, it isn't about what you do—it's when you do it. Time is his priority. That's why he may not plan a horse-and-carriage ride to Tavern on the Green right away. In fact, he'll schedule a casual first date, just to get the ball rolling as quickly as possible. As long as he gets the job done, accept with grace and enthusiasm. A simple, "That sounds like fun" will do. If he is a little shy and says something like, "Well, I was just wondering if you wanted to go out sometime?" Just say, "That sounds great. When were you thinking?" This isn't about how much money he has or how cool he is. This isn't about the first date being a big Saturday-night outing. It is about checking the box. Does he want to see you ASAP? If the answer is yes, then you should feel very flattered indeed.

What If He Doesn't Ask You Out on a Date ASAP?

There are some weird men who like to call women and chat on the phone. But they don't get around to setting up a date. Sometimes they will allude to a date at some future point by saying something like "Well, I'm going to be out of town until Wednesday so I'll call you when I get back and see if we can get together." This is the kind of man who, for whatever reason, feels no compelling reason to see you. If he wanted to see you, he would say, "Well, I'm going out to be out of town until Wednesday so are you free on Thursday?"

Don't make excuses for him. Why on earth would you want to be married to a man who can't figure out how to ask you on a date? If he can't ask you on a date right away, you will probably end up dating him for five years before he even thinks about proposing. Talk about a waste of time!

What kind of man likes to talk on the phone anyway? It is so much sexier if a man just gets to the point and schedules a date. To help this along, be friendly during his phone call, but don't be conversational. Allow some lulls so he can use them to ask you out. If, after a few niceties and some small talk, he hasn't asked you out—end the phone call or just allow enough lulls so that he ends the phone call. If he doesn't ask you out right away, on this first phone call, don't take any more phone calls from him. This may be hard, but it is for your own good.

He has one more chance to get it right if you stop taking his calls. He will need to ask you out by leaving a very specific message on your voice mail or answering machine. If he leaves a casual, "I just called to see what you are doing," or "Hey _____, it's _____, give me a call," forget about him. He needs to actually ask you out by saying something like, "Hey _____, it's _____. I wanted to see if you are free Thursday to go to dinner. Give me a call." If you receive a message like this, call him back. But don't be too excited. Be specific and tell him "I got your message about Thursday." This is his last chance; he needs to get right to the point and set up a date. No more talking! Let's hope that with all of the time he's had, he has something specific in mind. If he is casual about it and just wants to talk more, drop him right then and there. Just say:

"Listen, _____, I just don't think you and I are right for each other.
I think you need to find a woman who likes to talk on the phone more

than I do. I think you're a really nice guy but just not the guy for me. Fair enough? I really have to go."

Don't listen to his excuses. You gave him a couple of chances, and he blew it. If he is struggling at this early point, he won't make it through *The List*. If he can't ask you out for a cup of coffee, how in the heck is he going to ask you to marry him?

Long-awaited first dates are never good. A List Man is a man of action. He wants to see you. Talking on the phone is just the means to an end. Besides, if you are talking on the phone with him, there's nothing left to talk about on the date. Worst of all, you've become unreceptive to other dating opportunities. You have zeroed in on a man who isn't all that excited to see you.

How This Item Works for Online Dating

"Online dating" is a means of introduction, not a means of dating. Just because he owns a computer doesn't mean he is without a phone. Online dating may seem more complicated than traditional dating, but it really isn't when you have *The List*.

In "real" life, you have a better chance of meeting a quality man at a bookstore or at a friend's party than in a bar. Why? Because immediately you have something in common that doesn't have to do with booze or sex. In the same way, you will have a better chance of meeting a quality man online if you use an established online service that matches people according to their interests and values. These services charge a fee, but it is worth it. Signing up doesn't cost any more than a few glasses of wine, and it is an investment in your future.

Also, you know the man is serious about it since he has spent time filling out a values-based profile and has spent money subscribing. For a man, time + money = investment!

You will be asked to fill out a questionnaire that helps establish what you value in life and pinpoints your likes and dislikes. Questions will cover a range of topics from important value-based issues (such as how important developing a long-term relationship is to you) to personal preferences (such as what type of flowers you like the best). It will take time to answer the questions but this is a great activity, and remember: The men who subscribe to the site are going through the same process.

If you have to write a profile, make it reflect your personality and values. Don't waste time describing yourself in too much detail. Online, as in real life, he will approach you because he is attracted to you, not because you have a "great sense of humor" or like "long walks on the beach." Use the opportunity to describe what *he* is like. Use your list of Must Haves. Be brave! Here are some lines that may be helpful.

> ▷ You are looking for a wife, not another girlfriend.
> ▷ We both have friends but have been there done that. I am looking for a man who enjoys one-on-one time, not just hanging out with other people.
> ▷ I have a strong work ethic and so do you. But work isn't my life. I have time to share and so do you.
> ▷ You don't tell people you are a gentleman; you are a gentleman.
> ▷ You aren't a guy who plays games and only enjoys "the chase."

▷ You are a man of action. You know what you want and you
   go after it.
▷ If we are a match, I will be number one on your priority list
   and you will be number one on mine.

If you think these lines will scare men away, you are right. But
that is the point. Why waste time? There are many men who use
online dating to get attention or because they are bored. Let's face
it—for a man, online dating involves no risk. Because there is no risk
or rejection, there is little investment. You have to weed out the ones
who aren't serious. A List Man likes a woman who knows what she
wants and isn't afraid to say it. Post a flattering but realistic picture
of yourself. (Don't have any nieces, nephews, or children in your
picture—that's just too much.) And wait. A good site will make it very
easy for you by matching you with compatible men. A lesser quality
site will allow any man to contact you based on viewing your photo
and reading your profile. Either way, never e-mail a man first. If there's
a List Man out there in cyberspace, he will approach you. Most likely,
he will send you an automatic message to show you he is interested.
Best case (and the preferred *List* method), he will skip the automatic
message and send you a personal e-mail right away.

His initial e-mail should be all about you, not him (he knows you
have access to his profile). When a man uses the word "I" ten times in
a first e-mail, he is self-centered. If he wants a woman to respond, his
e-mail should read something like:

*"Wow! You are beautiful. I noticed that you also like _____. I would love to
meet you. Would you be comfortable giving me your phone number?"*

Believe it or not, some online men have form letters that they send to every woman who "winks" back at their automatic message. These letters will look like they are personal, but they aren't. The only way to tell if he really likes you is if he mentions something specific about your picture or your profile. If he sends an e-mail that is all about him, or sends a form letter, forget him. Use technology to block any more messages from him. He isn't a List Man.

After receiving a polite, personal e-mail, you can look at his picture and profile and see what you think. Hopefully, he will have posted a nice photo and will have a well-written profile. Ignore the guys who post more than two photos (at the gym, skiing, wearing a tuxedo) or write profiles that are boastful or self-centered. List Men don't need to show you photos of all the exciting places they have been and all the great outfits they own. A normal guy would be hard pressed to find one photo of himself, let alone six or seven. Besides, he doesn't want to be obnoxious or look like he is too into himself.

If you review his e-mail, picture, and profile, and you think he has potential, send him an e-mail that says:

> *"Thanks for the e-mail. My phone number is _____. Look forward to hearing from you."*

The List goes into effect, and he must call within twenty-four to forty-eight hours. Also, he needs to ask you out during your phone conversation. Just as if you have met him in "real life," he should take cues from you regarding your preference for a first date. Whether you decide on coffee, a drink after work, or a dinner out, he should choose a place that is convenient for you—not just the joint close to his office or apartment (where he meets all of his other online prospects). Meet him in a safe, public place, and take precautions that your friends know where you are when you are on the date. If he doesn't call, or calls and doesn't ask you out on a date, it is a sure sign he is spending his time on women he is more interested in. Don't even open any more of his e-mails. Just block him, delete his emails and forget him. If he is truly interested, he will call. A desperate woman will think, "Maybe he hasn't logged on." If he is serious about being involved in online dating, he should log on at least once a day. Besides, most reputable sites will tell you when he logs on, receives, and reads your message. If he doesn't log on daily, he is just doing online dating because he is bored.

ONLINE DATING MANDATES

1. **He only gets one e-mail from you—and that is in response to his polite, personal e-mail.** That way, you aren't establishing an e-mail relationship. If he is normal, he will want to escape the cyber weirdness and get into a normal routine of phone calls and dates.

2. **Your e-mail response is brief and includes your phone number.** You don't need to tell him all of your deep feelings or show him what a great intellectual you are. He has seen your picture. If he wants to know more, he needs to call and ask you out.

3. **Only open the first e-mail from him.** He has what he needs to talk to you and see you (duh, your phone number). If he doesn't use it, he is just some computer weirdo.

Mrs. Mary Corbett & Mrs. Sheila Corbett Kihne
Along with their publisher
Adams Media

Request the pleasure of your company at

"Find your Fairy Tale 2006"
A series of four, free live-chat sessions
hosted by the authors of The List

The first of February, May,
August, and November 2006 at
Seven o'clock in the evening, EST

RSVP
www.thelistformarriage.com for details

∽

Dinner and dancing will follow
at your wedding if you use The List

4. *The List* kicks into gear with the first phone call. He needs to call you within twenty-four to forty-eight hours and ask you on a date.

5. **Be safe.** Meet him in a public place. Tell your roommate or your friend where you are going, and give them a time when you will check in. Buy a book that teaches you how to be safe on dates.

Finally, online dating is one way to meet men. However, it should not be your only method. Unless you are on a site that matches you according to values, you will find that online dating produces quantity but not necessarily quality. Make sure that you are doing everything you can to "get out there" and meet quality men in other ways.

What If He Cancels the Date?

No List Man would ever dream of canceling a date. No matter what the reason, it couldn't possibly be worth hurting your feelings. More importantly, a List Man would never risk giving another man the opportunity to steal your heart while he is working late at the office. There may be legitimate reasons for bailing, but we sure can't think of any.

When Susan was single, an obnoxious man approached her at a bar. She was talking to her girlfriend and didn't appreciate the interruption. Susan was downright rude to him because she wanted him to go away. But her married friend thought that Susan should give him a chance and gave him Susan's number on the sly. After all, he was a good-looking lawyer and obviously liked her a lot.

He called the next day to ask Susan on a date. She accepted. However, on the night of the date, he called to cancel because he had an opportunity to take his daughter out to dinner. Susan knew very well that while this sounded noble, it was a strong indicator of where she would be on this man's priority list. She had her doubts initially, and this just nailed the coffin shut. He should have realized that he was on thin ice and kept the date.

When he called her again, she told him that she wasn't interested. She met her fiancé six months later. If she had started a relationship with this obnoxious man, she wouldn't have been available to meet her List Man.

If he likes you, you are his number-one project. Canceling a date (especially a first date!) during the earliest stages of dating is not behavior that will work with *The List*. Move on.

LIFE IN LISTOPIA

MEGAN

What a whirlwind weekend Megan has had! She's excited to finally have some new prospects. Although it's been six months since she dumped Colin, he creeps back in her mind from time to time, so she is relieved to have some new men to keep her on the straight and narrow. Although she wasn't initially attracted to Peter (the guy who approached her at the end of Saturday night's barbecue), she is still pleasantly surprised to hear from him on Wednesday evening when she returns home from the gym. He immediately says that he wanted to call her sooner, but it took some time to track down her phone number since he forgot to ask for her last name. He explains that he asked his friend Chad—who brought him to the function—if he knew who Megan was. Although Chad didn't, he knew one of the girls Megan was talking to. He had to call her for Megan's number, and Peter just got the information today. Peter jokingly says, "I hope you don't think I'm a stalker—I just thought our conversation was cut off too soon!" Megan clears her thoughts and tells him, "I'm sure my friend wouldn't pass my number along to a stalker—or a stalker's friend. Let's just say you are resourceful."

Since she puts him at ease, he immediately asks her if she'd like to go out to dinner on Friday night. Megan follows *The List* and replies with an enthusiastic "Yeah, definitely!" She still thinks he is a little nerdy over the phone but she figures that going out is better than staying in. Peter asks if she has any favorite restaurants, to which Megan replies, "Not really, I'm pretty open." He asks what her favorite food is, and she says, "Well, I really like just about everything."

She is a little bit annoyed by his less than take-charge performance, but it's too late to get out of it now. Peter proposes a new Thai restaurant in her neighborhood that he's heard about and asks her if it is okay to pick her up. She gives him her apartment address and tells him she will meet him in the lobby at 7:30 P.M. on Friday.

Meanwhile, she has not seen or heard from Drew, the man who approached her at the bar on Saturday. As tempting as the idea was, she swore that she would definitely not call him. The day after her call from Peter, she sees Drew in the lobby of the office building they share. He is busy chatting with coworkers and doesn't see her. He is really good looking, well dressed, and seems fun to be around.

Megan decides she really can't fault him for not calling because she didn't even give him her business card when he gave her his card. Maybe she'll make it a point to be in the lobby around the same time the next morning, or maybe she can figure out when he leaves for lunch and "accidentally" be in the same place. Just thinking about it makes her adrenaline rush. She decides to go to Saks and buy a cute new work outfit—maybe something in magenta. That will be sure to get his attention. After all, he is a good prospect and he did approach her at the bar that night and offer to buy her a drink, so she should at least make an effort not to avoid him.

She is interested in seeing Peter again, but at the same time Megan is *very* interested in the whereabouts of Drew.

TARA

Tara's online dating match, Patrick, has called her twice since getting her phone number three days ago. Although he called at prime times (between 7:00 and 9:30 P.M.), he wasn't able to reach her. He left one message on her machine, and his second call appeared on her Caller ID. She wanted to wait by the phone as *The List* advised, but she had been out of town at a two-day training seminar for work. She decides not to send him an e-mail, but calls him Thursday around 7:00 P.M. when she has some time to talk. Luckily she catches him and makes her apologies. Patrick quickly reassures her that it is okay and he is really glad to hear from her. They talk for about ten minutes about some of their experiences with the online dating service, and share some funny stories. Patrick says, "I know it is kind of last minute but if you don't have plans for the weekend, I would like to get together."

She tells him she is pretty open. She is curious to see if he will offer her the single woman's trophy—the Saturday-night date. He doesn't. Instead, he asks her if she wants to have lunch on Saturday. "Just like all the other online guys," Tara thinks to herself. But she agrees to meet him at a casual place in her neighborhood.

At long last! Bret calls Tara immediately upon his return from his business trip in China. It is almost 11:00 P.M. on a Thursday night, and she has a presentation in the morning, but he apologizes for the late call and explains that he is really mixed up from the jet lag. Bret starts out by paying Tara all of the compliments that their matchmaker Judy had told him about her. They talk for almost an hour. Bret is hilarious and has a really sexy phone voice. And since she has seen his picture online, Tara is feeling very hopeful indeed. They seem to have a lot in common as they are both from the Midwest, both fond of travel, and both tired of the singles scene. Tara is hoping the long conversation will lead to a date proposal. Bret explains that he has a ton of work to do over the weekend, but that he wants to meet her as soon as possible. He says he will call her Sunday and that they could get together for a nice dinner, maybe at the expensive French restaurant that he loves and desperately missed during his month abroad.

Tara is beside herself. Finally—a chance to wear her killer red Nicole Miller cocktail dress. Oh, and her lunch date with Patrick will be fun too. "Excellent work," she thinks.

CHRISTINE

Since Christine and Barry shared coffee after last Thursday's book-club meeting, he has called Christine every day. In fact, they've already spent three out of the last six nights doing something together. They've had pizza, watched a hockey game together on television, and done some shopping. After each date, they hug, and he sneaks a kiss on her cheek. Although she is really comfortable around Barry, she is very nervous about some things. She can't quite get over the fact that he is younger than she is and that he is a bit "underemployed." Also, she has noticed that his teeth are a little crooked. But to be fair, she finds herself smiling around Barry all the time. He is sweet, funny, and very "into" her feelings. He is fascinated with her job and quickly becomes acquainted with all the personalities in her office. He is always proactive in asking her about even the most mundane things. For a blue-collar guy, he has an amazing ability to really pick up on people's character traits and how they are wired. He tells her unbelievable stories about the characters he works with at the phone company. She finds herself just as interested in his job stories as he is in hers.

Their first "formal" romantic dinner date is set for Saturday night. Barry has made reservations at a nice restaurant downtown. She is both excited and apprehensive to see Barry in a different setting. She asks him what the attire is and he says, "You always know the right thing to wear, don't worry about it." Also, she feels bad because she knows how much the tab is going to be. But she decides to take one day at a time and not create problems that aren't really there.

To add to her confusion, Bill, her coworker and former crush, asks her out the day after she meets Barry. She notices that he is looking at her more and has made a point of inviting himself to a couple of group lunches that she is also invited to. After one of those lunches, he approaches her and starts talking about boats. She is completely confused but tries to pipe in with her limited knowledge of the subject. Finally, he segues to the annual boat show being held at the convention center that weekend and asks her if she wants to go with him. She thinks to herself quickly, "Well, I guess he approached me, and he is asking me out right away—on the spot, so this is a good thing." She gives him an enthusiastic "That sounds like fun." He even offers to pick her up at her home, which is in the opposite direction from where he lives.

She hasn't told Barry about the date—after all, they've only known each other for a week, so she figures she is not doing any harm. So why does she feel this nagging guilt? Hockey games and boat shows. Our corporate gal is really breaking out of her comfort zone!

WRAP-UP

So now your List Man has made the first move by approaching you, calling you at an appropriate time, and making plans to go on a date with you. Remember:

✅ If he calls right away but doesn't ask you out, he isn't worth your time. He may give good phone, but he isn't a man of action. If he doesn't ask you out during the phone call, don't take any more phone calls from him.

✅ If he failed to ask you on a date during your first phone conversation and you still want to give him another chance, the only thing he can do to save himself is ask you out by leaving a very specific message on your machine.

✅ Continue to be enthusiastic and encouraging to men who adhere to *The List*.

And, in regard to online dating:

✅ Online dating is just a tool of introduction.

✅ A quality online dating service that matches you based on values will produce the best results.

✅ Be on the lookout for self-centered men who use online dating because it is easy for them.

✅ If a man e-mails you and you think he has potential, you may e-mail him once. Then, *The List* goes into effect just as if you met in person.

✅ Online dating is one way to meet men but should not be your only strategy.

FIVE

List

Item 3:

HE MAKES
THE FIRST DATE
EASY AND FUN

Now for the fun part: the first date. It already feels relaxed and easy on your end because your List Man has scheduled a date ASAP, so you know he is interested in you. Hopefully, he has gathered enough information about you to know your preferences. Because he hasn't spent weeks trying to get to know you over the phone or via e-mail, you will have a lot to talk about.

First dates are unsuccessful when there is a delay between the first meeting and the actual date. Men who schedule the first date more than a few days out are giving you too much time to worry. The anticipation builds, and then the pressure is on. Because you and your List Man are seeing each other ASAP, you are swept up in the whirlwind and don't have time to overanalyze things.

What Is the Purpose of the First Date?

A man is attracted first to your physical appearance; the next item on his agenda is to make sure you ain't crazy. This is going to be tough because—let's face it—in a man's eyes we're all crazy. But don't worry. You have *The List*. You are feeling confident and in control, so you aren't going to come off crazy.

On your end, the only thing you need to accomplish on this date is to have fun and go with the flow. Above all, be yourself. If you are outgoing, be outgoing. If you are reserved, be reserved. If you like to drink—bottoms up! If you don't like to drink—bottoms up anyway. (Just kidding.) The point is that if you try to be somebody you aren't, it will eventually come back to haunt you. You are out with a man who may not even call you again, so don't let nerves or expectations keep you from relaxing and (at the very least) having fun.

While you should be yourself, don't be the "yourself" that you are on the phone with your sisters or your girlfriends (see "Crazy," at the beginning of this section). You don't need to completely overwhelm him with every detail of your life. It's just not polite conversation on a first date. Nobody is that interesting—not even you. Reality television would have us believe that it is important to talk about your deep feelings, fears, family issues, dreams, emotional barriers, Daddy issues, and last relationships when you first go on a date. It's usually better to stay off all those topics, but if it feels safe to tell him about your lifelong dream to quit your corporate job and become a professional ice-skater, then go ahead and talk about it. Don't be surprised if you are instantly comfortable with each other. While you don't need to get into anything too deep, it's common with a List Man to already be talking like you have been dating for some time. Go with the flow.

Caroline, the counselor introduced in List Item 1, met Justin, a police officer, at a church breakfast when she was twenty-six and he was twenty-seven. Caroline was impressed by his optimism and independence. They had their first date over lunch later that week. As she remembers, "We met at a busy restaurant and just clicked. We didn't get overly deep but our conversation was meaningful." Caroline didn't talk about wanting to marry Justin, but she didn't feel like she had to weigh her words or worry about scaring him off. She felt comfortable telling him, in general terms, what she was looking for in her life. She was herself and said what she felt like saying. They became inseparable immediately, talking on the phone daily until their second date. Both knew that there was a romantic attraction right away and they felt an even stronger urge to know each other as people. (PS: They were married a year later and have two sons ten years later.)

At this point, a List Man is way more interested in having fun with you than anything else. Of course, after he gets to know you more, he will love every bit of your personality, but you needn't deliberately expose your biggest flaws. Let the poor man have his little delusions at first. He will see you in rare form soon enough once you start flipping out over planning your wedding.

After he figures out that you aren't crazy, desperate, or damaged goods, the next thing he will do is try and find common ground with you. As one man says, "You are looking for things to agree upon."

First dates are about clicking. The chemistry he felt when he saw and approached you will either continue on your first date or it won't. Either way, there's nothing you can do besides relax and have a good time. If he is a List Man, he will give you every opportunity to shine.

Hopefully, conversation will flow easily—but this is not always the case. Even when there is a lull, you will feel at ease with a List Man. Try to help out as much as you can in this regard. He may be shy or afraid of turning you off. With luck, he will ask you some basic questions—not because he truly cares about your opinions on the state of the Middle East but because he is trying to keep the conversation going. He will ask you polite questions about your day, your weekend, and so on. He will inquire generally about your family and upbringing. If all goes well, he will figure out what you like to do for future date-planning purposes.

Sometimes women are so excited to be on a date that they disregard red flags. They feel that if the conversation is lively and they have tons to talk about, the date is a success. It's a successful date if you are feeling cherished, not challenged. If he is a List Man, he will not indulge in any of these no-no's:

▷ Try to debate with you
▷ Put you down
▷ Act superior
▷ Interview you
▷ Talk about himself too much
▷ Take a call on his cell phone (never, ever, ever!)
▷ Flirt with other women
▷ Invite other people to meet you during or after the date

You should follow the same rules of behavior. At the same time, the belief that a man loves you "as is" overrides anything you might do or say on a first date. If he is your List Man, he is madly in love with you from the start. He will think your ten extra pounds make you voluptuous. He will think your bad temper is cute. He will think your dumb stories are funny. Many first dates don't meet society's measure of a perfect first date, but they still result in happy marriages.

You will have a pretty good idea that you are with a potential List Man if you feel at ease. You won't feel like you have to impress him. You will see something in his eyes that makes you know he thinks you are amazing.

Here are some first-date tips from the panel of men we interviewed:

1. Exude confidence and charm.
2. Be a good listener.
3. Be laid back.
4. Be up on current events.
5. Be positive and polite to him and the people around you.

These are pretty basic requirements, and the lesson here is that this is just a first date. You will find out if he likes you for who you are soon enough. And if he doesn't, who cares? You've only invested a couple of hours in the fool anyway.

The He-Date

There is a very hard-to-recognize red flag that you must be aware of: the "He-date." *He* comes here all the time with his brother. *He* knows the maitre d'. *He* loves Jackie Chan movies. *He* thought it would be fun to go to the car show. Many men like to plan thinly disguised dates that are about their interests or ambitions.

Monica, a sophisticated urban woman, had a long-time crush ask her out to a tractor pull. Perhaps it was because he wanted to demonstrate his knowledge of tractors. Or maybe he thought he was being unique. Or maybe it was just really about his interests. He couldn't put aside his own preferences for one day and think about Monica's feelings. He probably figured that if there wasn't chemistry, at least he still got to do something he enjoyed.

Andrea went out with a very promising man who made the first move and called right away to set up a date. These positive actions were enough to make her overlook the fact that he was wearing a suede overcoat . . . in June . . . in Atlanta. But what she couldn't overlook was his plan to be "different" by expecting her to take public transit to and from the date, even though there had been recent muggings on the system, and even though he drove a BMW. *He* took her on the train because *he* thought it would be clever to tell her how *his* grandparents had met on a train fifty years ago. Like this was a luxury Zephyr in Europe or something! She felt very vulnerable in her Betsey Johnson sundress and strappy heels. She decided to spend her next Friday night on a first date with a really nice guy who had talked to her enough to figure out her favorite foods. They went out for sushi. (PS: He proposed four months later, and they are married now and expecting their first child.)

Julie seemed to continually date "He-men." After weeks of cat and mouse, Lance, an attractive ophthalmologist, finally asked Julie out. He decided to take her to church (they were both of the same religion) and to brunch at his favorite eatery (a very expensive and lavish location). She thought that this was a very special first date. After brunch, he didn't want the date to end. He asked her if she wanted to drive to a really hoity-toity gated community where he was looking at "estates." He drove her around on a golf cart and showed her million-dollar suburban mansions.

Even though they had a great time (or at least she did), he didn't call for a long time. Rather than spending his time asking about Julie's life, Lance spent his time showing off what a good guy he was and that he knew all the best things to order on the menu. But, most importantly in Lance's mind, he showed her that he was a rich doctor who could buy a million-dollar house. Once Julie had *The List,* she realized that she'd lived through the mother of all He-dates and moved on. Amen!

Many a dolt on the show *A Dating Story* has taken an unsuspecting woman to his family farm to sit on a hay bale and look at cows. And isn't it charming that the guy dominates the episode, talking about how special this place or that place is to him? This is to be expected of a jackass who would agree to strut his stuff on television. But in the real world, this is risky. What type of man plans a date around his own interests and history? An egomaniac, that's who. Women will think to themselves "Wow, he's sharing all this with me; I must be the one." But that's unlikely. He should be more interested in finding out about you and pleasing you than in talking about himself. How can he really do that if he's showing off? You don't want a guy who thinks he's a great catch; you want a guy who just *is* a great catch. Don't talk yourself into thinking that these kinds of dates are cute and original. They aren't. They are just plain selfish.

A List Man would never risk turning you off by taking you someplace too unconventional. Any man over the age of eighteen should know that dinner and a movie is always safe and stylish. A List Man knows that women like to dress up cute and be seen out on dates and that a first date is not a "test" to see how you fit into his world. After you are engaged will be the time for him to reveal the workings of his inner nerd.

A man who makes it about himself from the get-go won't make a good husband. He is the type of man who, when asked what he loves about you, will say things like:

- ▷ "She is always there for me."
- ▷ "She takes care of me."
- ▷ "She makes me feel good about myself."
- ▷ "She loves me for who I am."

A List Man, on the other hand, would say things like:

▷ "She's gorgeous and smart and funny."
▷ "She's got a great heart and a great sense of humor."
▷ "She's a caring, loving person with a zest for life."

Do you see the difference? A List Man is centered on you—not himself. That's why if the date is centered on *his* hobbies, *his* interests, *his* favorite restaurant (that he takes every date to), or *his* house for dinner, it is about him and not about you. Proceed with caution.

List Man Actions on the First Date

Once you're sure you're clearly not on a He-date, there are some actions a man will take on a first date that are strong indicators that you are off to a good start:

▷ He will be on time and on the lookout for you if you are meeting him at a certain spot.
▷ He will be focused on you. (This means he won't flirt with the waitress, conveniently "find" his friends in the restaurant, or strike up a conversation with the people at the next table.)
▷ He will ask if you want a drink if you have to wait for a table.
▷ He will pick up the tab, and you will let him.

There is a lot of debate about the last item of the List Man Action items above—picking up the tab versus going Dutch. If you're following *The List*, it's a must have. "Easy and fun" means: easy and fun for *you*. There is nothing fun about sitting in uncomfortable silence waiting for somebody to grab the tab. The quality—and not the scale—of the experience is what matters most. A List Man will plan a date that he can afford and budget accordingly. Even if you are just meeting for a quick cup of coffee, a List Man will wait until you arrive to place his order. That way, he can pick up the tab for both. Even if your dinner date gets extended to include after-dinner drinks at another location, or your brunch date evolves into catching a spur-of-the-moment movie, he will pick up the tab for every "segment" versus "taking turns." Why does he need to pick up the tab? Because:

1. He doesn't want there to be any awkwardness, and is there anything more awkward than fumbling around to pay a check? (We've all been in these situations with girlfriends—"But I didn't drink and only ordered a baked potato!" You don't want to deal with this on a date.) He doesn't want to cause you any discomfort or embarrassment.

2. He knows that a gentleman picks up a tab and sees this as something he can do for you right away. He wants to take care of you. More importantly, he wants to be in control. Career women may have a hard time with this, but you can split the bill after you're engaged.

3. He isn't counting. Numbers aren't on his mind. He doesn't expect you to buy the popcorn just because he bought dinner and movie tickets. The only thing he cares about is making things easy and comfortable for you.

Don't be tempted to pull out your credit card because you're scared he won't offer to pay and it will be uncomfortable or ruin a great date. Let the check hang out there. If he doesn't pick up the tab quickly, it usually means one of the following:

▷ **Best case:** He's a cheapskate. And if this is what he is, don't *ever* pull out your wallet. Make him ask you to split the bill—serves him right. If you are also a cheapskate (the kind who brags about being completely debt free and will only pay for exactly your share), then this may be a match made in heaven.

▷ **Worst case:** He is openly telling you this is a casual moment for him and he isn't diving in too fast. You aren't important enough for him to impress. Obviously, after meeting you in person and talking to you on the phone, he isn't "sold" yet. Obviously, he has time to waste—but you don't!

The Never-ending Date

Many of the happily married couples say their first date almost seemed "never ending." There was no need to cut it off to play hard to get. Coffee turned into lunch. Lunch turned into shopping. Shopping turned into dinner, which turned into a late night. If a List Man makes a lunch date with you but has to pick his dog up from the groomer later that afternoon, he may say something like, "I don't suppose you'd want to come along?" Or he will take care of the errand and then meet you as soon as he can. This is the beginning of being inseparable.

So how will a date with a List Man end? If you are with a List Man, and if you have definitely set off his Alarm, you will leave the first date with a smile on your face because you know he will call you.

Not just because he said he would—but because he will end the date by trying to pin you down on when he can see you next. He will make plans for your next date by saying something very specific like, "I'll call you tomorrow to make plans for the weekend." Don't be surprised if he can't even wait another day to see you again. Plenty of List Men have left a lunch date and called a couple of hours later to see if they could get together that same evening.

A List Man *doesn't* end a date by saying, "I had a great time. Is it okay if I call you again?" Or, "I'll give you a call." Sure, any guy can take you out for a good time. But how easy is it for you if he sets you up to wait and wonder by the phone?

With a List Man, you will never have an insecure thought pass through your head. The end of the date won't seem like an ending —but a beginning. The whole process—from the beginning—is flawless and easy.

LIFE IN LISTOPIA

MEGAN

Peter is right on time for Megan's date. He picks her up in a little red sports car that looks to be at least a dozen years old. It's cute, and she can tell that he just had it washed (inside and outside), but she's really starting to wonder what he does for a living. Peter looks as fresh scrubbed as his car, sporting a checked button-down and khakis. No flowers, but he does open the door for her wherever they go.

The conversation in the car is friendly, and they take the opportunity to get to know each other. Peter asks all kinds of questions about Megan's job in the banking industry. She tries to explain that she's just a loan processor and it's pretty boring, but Peter thinks it sounds interesting and asks her detailed questions about the deals she works on, interest rates, and leasing verses buying. He laughs at her stories about crabby customers, weird bosses, and troubled coworkers. He asks her about her family, her interests, and her favorite things to do. Megan has a good time talking about herself for the first part of the date. She even shares with him her dream of some day owning a flower shop. She's not sure why she feels this comfortable on a first date; usually she'd try to play the part of "career girl" a little bit better.

After dinner arrives, Megan turns the subject to Peter. He is twenty-eight years old from a small town in Oklahoma, and he moved to attend medical school. He's an anesthesiology resident with fewer than two years of training to go. Megan's only exposure to the medical field is via reruns of *ER,* but she is very impressed that he's going to be a doctor. This explains his complete lack of a tan! He goes on to explain that he went to the barbecue with his friend to try to meet some people outside of medicine, as that is who he spends all of his time with and "it gets really boring" talking shop all day.

He's had a couple of girlfriends, one in college, one in medical school, but doesn't elaborate. He makes it obvious that they were not serious relationships and that he is baggage-free. He doesn't have much of a life outside of work right now, but he likes computer games and science-fiction movies. He throws in a few self-effacing jokes about never attending a *Star Trek* convention and trying to limit his game-playing to three hours a night.

Although Megan doesn't think they have a ton in common, she does think that his humility is refreshing. She loves how he takes such interest in her life and laughs at her (sometimes mean) stories about annoying people in her life. He's shy but smart, and she feels very at ease with him. She feels comfortable—so much so that she suddenly realizes that although they ordered a bottle of wine for both of them, she has had most of it herself. Megan is a light drinker and knows that she will regret her overindulgence in the morning.

When the tab comes, Peter immediately grabs it. Megan expresses concern, since he's a resident, and suggests splitting the bill. "Stop," he says good-naturedly, "I've got it covered." End of story. When he walks her to the door, he asks when he can see her again. "I don't suppose you're free tomorrow?" Megan is feeling a little out of sorts. She is starting to break out in a cold sweat. She knows that it is the wine and tries as hard as she can to hold herself together until she gets inside. "Are you okay?" he asks.

"I just . . . I think I had too much wine."

He replies, "Aw, we didn't have that much. Sometimes it just hits you the wrong way." He helps her up to her apartment. She apologizes and he continues to downplay the situation. He gets her a glass of water, and settles her on the couch. The next thing she knows it's morning. She is horrified and suffering not only a physical hangover, but a social hangover as well. She starts replaying things that she said to Peter and winces thinking about what a dunce he must think she is. "Way to impress the doctor," she thinks to herself. She walks into her bathroom and finds a sticky note on her mirror. It has a smiley face with an arrow pointing down to a bottle of aspirin, it says: "Take two of these and call me in the morning."

Megan grins from ear to ear. She is feeling better already. By the time she is out of the shower and ready to call Peter, he beats her to the punch. He tells her that he had a great time last night and glosses over the hairy part. He nonchalantly asks her what she is doing with her day, and she tells him she is going to a wedding shower. He tells her that he is on call at the hospital for the day but wonders if she can catch a movie Sunday afternoon. She tells him she's free and they confirm the details of the date.

At the wedding shower, Megan can't help but think about Peter. She's still not sure how attracted she is to him, but she is very excited about seeing him the next day. She is smiling without realizing it! Their movie date on Sunday is easy and fun. They decide to forgo lunch for popcorn and candy. She doesn't care if he sees her pig out and thinks, "What a weird thing to not care about so early on." She is thankful that he picked a movie without a ton of sex scenes in it. It is a light romantic comedy, and she enjoys it completely. His arm touches hers on the armrest and she notices every sensation. They lean close and whisper to each other.

When Monday morning rolls around, Megan is thinking about her weekend with Peter. After the movie, they grabbed an early dinner. Then he came over to her place and hung out. He even called her before she went to bed. But now it is time for work and back to reality.

As she waits for her elevator at work, Drew approaches her. (Must be the magenta dress.) "Hey there! I've been looking for you. I've been waiting by the phone for your call. Why didn't you call me?" he jokes, as if he is a woman scorned.

"I must have lost your card," she replies coolly as she steps into the elevator.

He follows her in. "Well, it serves me right. I'm a jerk for thinking a girl like you needs to chase guys. I should have gotten your number that night." She lifts her eyebrows at him and smiles. "Are you free for lunch today? Nobody has lunch plans on Monday," he says pointing to her lunch bag.

"Well, you're right about that. Sounds great." He tells her to meet him in the lobby and they will go from there.

She takes the date and they have a nice lunch flirting and joking about the business world. She learns that Drew is the youngest sales manager at his company and that he manages ten reps. He puts down the finance people at his company as "inept morons who couldn't close a deal to save their lives." She smiles. He's lucky she isn't the sensitive type or she might have been offended. She goes along with it and before you know it lunch hour is past. Drew throws down his corporate credit card to pay the bill and says, "I've got a one o'clock. I'll give you a call later." He asks for her phone number and e-mail address. She gives him her card, and he sticks it in his wallet without looking at it. He dashes off and leaves her at the hostess stand.

She watches him walk away and thinks once again, "Wow, is he hot or what?" And he was so sarcastically funny. Back at her desk, she is distracted. She can't think about anything besides Drew. They definitely have a lot in common. They both like to work out. They both like to go out to trendy bars and restaurants. They are both into clothing. They seem to be at the same place in their lives.

Her thoughts are interrupted by a call from Peter. He has a busy week planned at the hospital so she won't be able to see him until later in the week. Late in the afternoon, she receives an e-mail from Drew (as part of a personal distribution list) with a really funny attachment about work personality types.

On Wednesday, she has a really nervous feeling in her gut. It has been years since she had felt it. She recognizes it from her early days with Colin. She is waiting for Drew to call her. With every hour that passes, she feels more nervous and more upset. By 4:00 P.M. on Thursday afternoon, she is downright livid. She has heard nothing from Drew. She swore to herself that she would never get wrapped up in this type of thing again! Here she barely knows the guy and she is feeling all of the familiar emotions that she had felt with Colin! Just as she is getting ready to leave the office early (she can't sit there anymore—she is too distracted and upset), Drew calls. "Hey! What's up?" she mumbles something back. "Say, I know this is last minute, but what about meeting me for a drink after work?"

She replies, "I'm leaving early—in fact, I was just on my way out."

He says, "Hey, that works for me. I'm nothing if I'm not easy." She agrees to meet him for a drink. At the bar, she decides to be smart and just order soda. She wants to impress Drew and keep her wits about her. She also wants to make him squirm a little bit for not calling sooner. He isn't going to have the advantage of loosening her up with a drink. He notices she isn't drinking and tries to coax her to have "just one." She stands her ground. Within the hour, a group of Drew's coworkers joins them. Megan has a great time with the gregarious salesmen and likes being the center of attention. With five Diet Cokes in her, she is feeling pretty wired. Drew walks her to her car and they kiss. It is a good kiss, and she feels it in her toes.

When she finally gets in her car, it is nearly 7:00 P.M. She notices two missed calls on her cell phone. She completely forgot that she had told Peter she'd meet him at 6:00 P.M. for an early dinner. Her head is spinning. She contemplates just making up a little white lie so Peter won't be hurt. She justifies her actions in her mind. She wants to get married and she needs to keep all of her options open. She had been so sure that Colin was "the one" for her and wasted a lot of time waiting for him. She isn't going to be tricked by either Drew or Peter. Peter will just have to understand where she is.

TARA

When Tara meets Patrick for lunch, she is pleasantly surprised to see that he is much taller than his online picture made him look. He has a mop of curly black hair and is cute in his up-to-date jeans and fashionably untucked striped shirt. He has a nervous laugh, and she notices that his eyebrows are really bushy, but other than that he seems like he is far enough to the right on the evolution chart.

Initially, they continue where their brief phone conversation left off. They chat more about the online dating experience, and Patrick says that although he just signed up, he's already overwhelmed at the amount of matches he's had. But he's quick to point out he only called her. He says that he liked her smile and her big blue eyes. He also likes that her profile stated she enjoys running, but more importantly that she shares the same political and religious views as he does. He explains that at thirty-three, he feels he is too old to debate these subjects. He knows what he thinks and he is only interested in marrying someone with similar values.

Tara hasn't thought about this quite so plainly before. She has dated so many types of men and never felt that she had to be with somebody just like her. But, then again, none of those relationships had panned out.

Tara tells Patrick that she's been on the dating service for a year. She says she was about to let the subscription expire since it really hadn't brought any quality men into her life, but that she was intrigued Patrick called so soon after receiving her number. She adds that it was hard for her to make the transition from online to in-person and that she doesn't want to dwell on how she had met somebody. He agrees, "Yeah, it is really weird. There is a part of you that thinks that you are too good for online dating. But everybody does it. The key is to escape the weirdness as soon as possible." She couldn't have said it better. He picked up her cue. They never discuss online dating again.

Tara leads the conversation by asking Patrick about his life. She learns that he has a degree in business and manages his family's small chain of local golf shops. He works typical retail hours and basically is a "jack of all trades." He does everything from accounting to buying. He likes to golf (but when he notices her lack of enthusiasm, he quickly notes that he doesn't have much time for it). Patrick is hard for Tara to peg. Even though he works in the suburbs, he lives in the city. He collects both military history books and comic books. He loves obscure local alternative bands but also names a fifty-year-old piano bar as his favorite place to hang out. He is a unique person—she can't really fit him into any stereotype.

During their conversation, Patrick says that he doesn't see any point in wasting time and that when he sees something, he goes after it. She likes his intensity and frankness. He asks Tara questions about her life, but mostly he listens. He listens as she talks about her goal to run in a marathon, her screwed-up-yet-still-married parents, and her fast-paced job.

Two hours pass, and dessert is long gone. They decide to continue their date. They catch an afternoon movie and then before they go their separate ways, he asks her if he can call her the next day. He doesn't even wait that long. Her phone is ringing as soon as she walks in the door. He doesn't even make an excuse for calling her. They talk for a while, and he tells her that he has a problem to resolve at work. He asks if she would be interested in going to the piano bar for a nightcap later that night. She thinks that sounds perfect. She takes a nap and spends an extra-long time getting ready for her date. She picks up her place and runs out to the local market to buy fresh flowers, a bottle of wine, and some gourmet cheeses. By the time Patrick arrives—looking very cleaned-up and elegant in his all-black ensemble—she has everything set to go. They linger at her place and almost don't want to leave. Patrick jokes that they had better move on before she slaps him for moving too fast. They have a blast at the piano bar and kiss heavily on her couch when they return. Patrick leaves her house at 2:30 A.M. It is the longest, easiest first date in the history of first dates.

Sunday morning comes and Tara begins having second thoughts. She looks up Patrick's profile online and examines his photo closely. He is sort of weird looking. She can't quite put her finger on it, and she isn't sure what her girlfriends will think of him. She starts to regret all the kissing and wishes she had done some things differently. She has never taken the time to complete her list of "must haves." She knows what she wants, and she just doesn't think Patrick has the "it" factor. Her thoughts are interrupted by a phone call from Bret.

She had almost forgotten about him! They're supposed to have dinner that night. She is grateful that they have plans because it will give her a convenient excuse not to see Patrick. This is another thing about Patrick—he seems so available.

Bret is polite and pleasant as he tells her that he is really sorry, but he can't get together that night. He is under the gun to finish some schematics that are due for a client presentation on Monday. He wants to take her out on a night when he can relax and focus on getting to know her, and he also thinks a Saturday night might be more fun than Sunday anyway. So he says he'll call her at the end of the week, but that she should keep next Saturday open, because he "definitely" wants to take her to that favorite French restaurant of his.

Tara is disappointed. The whole date with Patrick seems kind of yucky now. She can't believe she kissed him so much. She decides she is done with online dating. When Patrick calls to ask her about getting together that day or night, she lies and tells him she has already made plans with a girlfriend. He tries to talk to her in—what seems to her— too intimate a way. She quickly tells him that her neighbor's dog has just run into her yard and she has to catch him. He sounds confused but tells her that he will try her later.

She looks at her red dress on the hanger and figures she'll get to wear it soon enough. Bret is much more her type physically and he has a cool job. Patrick has a boring job and seems a little desperate. Tara crawls back into bed to watch television for a few hours. That night, she orders pizza and debriefs the weekend's activities with her girlfriends on the telephone.

CHRISTINE

Barry and Christine never had a technical "first date," as everything has been pretty casual thus far. They have dinner plans for Saturday night, but she still keeps the plans to make the boat show with Bill on Saturday afternoon. When Barry calls Saturday morning to see if she wants to grab coffee and go check out some open houses in the neighborhood, she tells him she has to take her grandmother out to lunch. She can tell he is disappointed. She doesn't need to see his face to know the expression on it. She knows that she made the right decision to make up a little white lie. She begins to realize that Barry is probably falling for her. In the meantime, Bill calls her to tell her that he is running late. He starts to explain but—troubleshooter that she is—she jumps in and offers to meet him at the convention center for the boat show. He puts up a weak fight but then agrees that she is a "lifesaver."

When she arrives at their designated meeting spot at the convention center, Bill isn't there. She spots him inside the convention hall. She pays for her ticket and walks into the event. He waves her over and she sees that he isn't alone. He has brought Emily, his nine-year-old daughter, along. She is annoyed. Although she likes kids and wants to have her own children, she just isn't prepared to spend the day balancing adult conversation with kid conversation. She knows from her nieces that nine can be a really annoying age.

Bill seems very happy to see her and says, "Boy, you look great." She is dressed head to toe in fashionable black. She stands out regally from the scads of other women sporting pleated pants and fanny packs. "So how 'bout we grab a hot dog?" Bill offers. Emily whines about wanting something else instead, and he tries to catch Christine's eyes in an "Isn't she cute" kind of way. She purposely avoids his glance.

As they walk from boat to boat (who knew there were so many boats?), Bill puts his hand on the small of her back. Emily takes notice. "I think you're going to get married," she taunts Christine. Again, Bill smiles at his daughter's wit and verve. Christine says nothing. To cover the awkwardness, he starts rambling on about how she will grow up and be a great lawyer, or prophet, or this or that. His diatribe ends with "I swear, the kid's clairvoyant."

"Well, then she can probably predict I'm outta here," Christine thinks to herself. She can't even wait to finish the last aisle of yachts. She makes an excuse and leaves. She is so glad that she has driven herself. She says her goodbyes and makes her way toward the parking ramp.

When Christine gets home, she rushes to get ready for her date with Barry. He picks her up and compliments her dress and they head off to a nice Italian restaurant that Christine chose. Barry seems a little out of spirits. She hopes that he isn't put off by the posh restaurant. She is surprised that Barry knows a lot about wine. After talking politely with the sommelier, he orders a nice bottle of cabernet. After the wine arrives, Barry makes a toast to Christine. He smiles at her and calmly says: "So, what did Granny think of the boat show?"

She nearly chokes. Barry sits back and enjoys watching the always-cool Christine squirm. He tells her his brother dragged him to the show last minute and he saw her with a date and a little girl. "I'm not trying to make you uncomfortable; I know you have every right to see who you want."

She tries to explain herself. He only replies, "I know, it's been a quick thing but I don't feel any need to see anybody but you."

Rather than use her lawyer skills to reason with him that she doesn't feel they are exclusive yet so another date was okay, she decides to take another course. She can't help herself because when she looks at Barry across the table, she feels what her happily married friends have always tried (in vain) to explain to her. She knows that he is the one for her, and she also knows that he feels the same way. They are so different, and they barely know each other. But he is the man she has been looking for her whole life.

For the first time in her life, Christine begs. "I don't know what I was thinking. He asked me out before I really knew. But I do know. I want to be with you. I don't think I realized that until right now but that's how I feel. You have to forget about this. Please forgive me."

He reaches for her hand and says, "You know I'm in this for the long haul."

By the end of their dinner, only two weeks after their first meeting at the bookstore, they are excitedly discussing when they will get engaged and when they will get married. They laugh together about how shocked their family, friends, and coworkers will be. Bill will probably faint. And as for little Emily, Christine has to agree with Bill—the kid does have an uncanny ability to see the future.

WRAP-UP

It is likely that the first date with your List Man will last a long time. The first date should be easy and fun. Fun means fun for *you*. Easy means that you should never have a moment to consider you won't see him again. Because *The List* is all about the List Man's actions, these are the requirements:

☑ He should make you feel special by asking you questions about yourself.

☑ He should refrain from bragging about himself too much.

☑ He should plan something that you are comfortable with and not make the date about him.

☑ He should pick up the tab without hesitation.

☑ He should leave you in no doubt that you will see each other very soon.

SIX

List

Item 4:

HE CALLS YOU WITHIN
TWENTY-FOUR HOURS TO
SET UP SUBSEQUENT DATES—
THEY ARE EASY, FUN,
AND ONE-ON-ONE

For a lot of couples whose first date falls into the "never-ending" category, this List item may not even apply because they are already inseparable. For these couples, the structured "phone call" phase is over. However, not every List Man can leap tall buildings in a single bound. Mere mortal List Men may need a little more time.

In the same way that he called you ASAP to ask you out the first time, the List Man will keep the momentum building by calling you daily to set up subsequent dates. He certainly doesn't get forty-eight hours to ask you out again. Two days would be an impossible eternity to wait—for a man who is crazy about you. He has had a chance to see what you are all about. Either he:

1. **Really likes you,** in which case he will call within twenty-four hours (at the most). He wants to keep things moving at a fast clip. He has your attention and knows that it isn't smart to play games.
2. **Likes you enough,** in which case he will call within a couple of days to ask you out again. He may want you to be his girlfriend but not his wife. You definitely haven't sounded The Alarm.
3. **Doesn't like you,** in which case he won't call. For whatever reason, the chemistry isn't there. Don't worry about it. You haven't invested any time in him, so who cares? Try not to dwell on it.

Assuming that he has met you and decided quickly that you are quite the catch, what is his little monkey-man brain thinking?

1. He knows the odds of meeting somebody like you again are slim to none.
2. He doesn't want to let anybody else have a chance with you.
3. He thinks you have men beating down your door and wants to eliminate competition by filling up your dance card.
4. He wants to be a part of your life.
5. He knows that if he can talk to you, he will stay on your mind.
6. He wants to see you right away because he misses you.

If you have sounded The Alarm, he will have no shame. He will want to see you right away, usually within a day or two of your first date. As with List Item 2, the second date will occur at <u>your</u> earliest convenience.

He Prefers One-On-One Dates

From the start, you are all he needs. He doesn't need other distractions to make things fun or interesting. Other people are just a nuisance during the first few months of dating. After you are married, you will have a social circle to keep life interesting, but you'll still both be completely happy hanging out one-on-one together.

If a man wants you to fit into a schedule of happy hours with coworkers, attending his friends' parties, or going on group dates with other couples, he may be more interested in being part of a couple than in getting married. There is a big difference, and this is the time to take notice of how he wants to interact with you. Even though it is fun to have a full calendar and to have fun plans with the man you are interested in, you don't want a man who is only looking for a girlfriend. You want a man who is looking for a wife.

In the early stages of dating, many women think that when a man sweeps her up into his social circle and vice versa, they must be well on the way to serious commitment. This may be true. But this commitment is nearly always boyfriend/girlfriend versus husband/wife. It's dangerous when women entwine their social lives with a man this early in *The List*. Women who merge their social lives with men too early are depriving themselves of being wooed.

Darcy has been dating her "boyfriend" Jason for three years. Right out of the gate, they spent their time with friends at bars, with friends at concerts, with friends at parties. Then they spent their time going to their friends' wedding showers, weddings, baby showers, and baptisms. Still, they remained boyfriend/girlfriend. Darcy experienced the short-term high of being introduced in public as Jason's girlfriend. But they never built a very romantic connection. It was very difficult for Darcy to finally break it off with Jason because their social lives were so dependent on each other. Worse yet, she still bumped into him every now and then, and there was no hope of meeting a new man within her social circle because it was also Jason's social circle. Darcy made a fresh start and met a List Man. She realized how wonderful it is to be Number One in a man's eyes!

The first thirty days are the "cocooning time," during which he wants you all to himself. You should feel the same way. He is focused on getting to know you and creating intimacy with you. Courtship is a precious time—don't wish it away because you are too anxious to be a public couple. Being around other people adds another layer of stress. The more outside people present in a social situation, the less someone will act like himself or herself.

If a man wants to bring you into his social circle too soon, coyly tell him: "Well, that does sound fun, but I would rather just be with you."

A List Man will be delighted by this and take your cue. Don't worry about missing any big events. A List Man will—of course—invite you to any mandatory obligations that occur (including work functions, formal events, or weddings) during courtship. If he isn't a List Man, he will quickly grow restless and stop calling. Put him to the test!

As far as his friends go, here's a little secret: When a man wants to marry a woman, his friends, if he has a lot of friends, go by the wayside. He knows that friends who have their heads on straight understand that this is the way things are. It is an unwritten rule among good men that the woman comes first.

Women need deep connections with other women. Women like to share their problems and commiserate together. Men aren't like this. In fact, many wonderful men don't have a lot of friends. Or, if they do, their friends serve a casual function in their life while they look for their future wife. A List Man depends on his wife for emotional support. This is the primary relationship in his life. He may like to go out and golf once in a while or play video games—but it's never to get away from you. It is to clear his head so he can relax. There is nothing more pleasing to a woman than to be truly needed. The best marriages have this healthy "codependence," and evidence of it is present even in the early stages of dating.

Of course, there are the men who will never dump their friends for you because to them it is more important that life be a nonstop party than any sort of spiritual journey. If you do end up marrying a man who is Mr. Fun, just know that he will expect a thriving social life. Eventually, if you decide to have children, the party's definitely over—for you. A lot of married men of this type love to extend their out-of-town trips to get away from their families, go out to dinner, and drink and socialize with friends. But when you are married, working full time, running a household, and/or raising children—you had better identify fun with each other because there won't be time or energy to seek it from outside sources. Who wants a man who is antsy and sulks around because things aren't fun all of the time? No thanks!

You don't need to be locked up in a castle tower with no social life. Once you determine he is a List Man, you can certainly "go public" as a couple. Because you have established an intimate connection with each other, and haven't had to deal with pressure from friends and family members, this will be a meaningful and natural step.

What If He Doesn't Call Within Twenty-four Hours of the First Date?

There are few dating occurrences more heartbreaking than expecting a phone call after a great first date and not getting it. Why does this happen? Try to remember a time when this happened to you. You'll probably notice that even though the date went well, he may have not clearly checked the boxes prior to the first date. Maybe you actually approached him. Or maybe he waited more than twenty-four to forty-eight hours to call you, or wasted time leaving messages on your voice mail instead of talking to you directly. Maybe he didn't schedule a date right away, or maybe the first date was more about him debating you than pleasing you.

How many times have you blamed yourself when you assessed a dating relationship and wondered why it wasn't moving toward courtship? You thought you were too needy, too reserved, that you opened up too fast, that you didn't open up fast enough, or that you should have played hard to get. What a bunch of garbage this is! He failed to call after the first date because he was not your List Man. It was nothing you said or did or didn't do. It has nothing to do with your "baggage." Even if you said too much or acted a little crazy, if you are the one, you can do no wrong. If a man loves you and is courting you, he will love you for exactly who you are. So don't waste time thinking you did anything wrong. You didn't. If you are the one for him, he won't care if:

- ▷ You are divorced.
- ▷ You want five kids.
- ▷ You have five kids.
- ▷ You have a stupid job.
- ▷ You make twice as much money as he does.
- ▷ You slept with him on the first date.
- ▷ You want to stay a virgin until you're married.
- ▷ You drank too much.
- ▷ You didn't drink at all.
- ▷ You slipped in an f-bomb or two during polite dinner conversation.
- ▷ You grew up in Dysfunction Junction.

For mysterious reasons that cannot be explained or controlled, he wants you just as you are.

When a man seems to be a List Man and fails to call after the first date, it is hard to understand and accept. What happened? There are a few possible reasons:

1. **He isn't ready.** Maybe he saw you and thought that he was, but he isn't. He went on the first date with good intentions, but maybe your classy manners or positive aura intimidated him because he realized you're not going to settle for just sleeping with him. He is not ready for marriage, and you can't make him ready. Don't waste time thinking that "He's just scared."

2. **There is somebody else.** Men are selfish by nature. It's likely that:
   - He already has a girlfriend (or wife even!). He can't resist you because you are new, but when it really comes down to being a man and breaking off a current relationship, he won't do it.
   - He has had his eye on a woman for a while, and she is suddenly available.
   - A woman from his past has come back into the picture.

3. **He changed his mind.** The chemistry that he felt when he first saw you fizzled on his end—even if it increased on yours. He decided that you weren't the one for him. Don't take it personally because it doesn't matter.

Don't dwell on the "why." You didn't sound The Alarm and there is nothing you can do about it. It doesn't matter because you're never going to talk to him or see him again. Just know that it is one or a

combination of the reasons above, and move on. If a man calls after
the deadline of the post-first-date phone call, use the same response
as for List Item 2:

> *"You know, _____, after I go out with a guy on a date, I expect him
> to call me right away to ask me out again. I only go out with guys who
> really pursue me, and I can tell this if they call within a couple of days."*

Even if he offers complete contrition for not calling, he has still
just missed an item on *The List,* and it is highly unlikely that this will
be the man you marry. If he tries to make you feel stupid, in any way,
brush him off. Give him the same line from List Item 2:

> *"I'm really sorry. You have your own way of doing things, and I have my
> way. And I only go out with guys who call me quickly. You can think
> whatever you want to, but that's just how I am. Let's just leave it at
> that. Goodbye and good luck!"*

Easy and Fun Continues

The second half of this List item is simply a repeat of List Item 3: All
subsequent dates are easy and fun. Even if the first date perfectly
conformed to *The List*, there is still a chance that this guy will screw
up in a major way and decide that it now seems appropriate to have
you pick up the check, take you to a concert featuring his favorite rock
band (even though he now knows you like jazz), or invite his two best
friends along on your second or third date. All the same rules apply as
outlined in the previous List item. There is no wiggle room!

LIFE IN LISTOPIA

MEGAN

Even though Peter is doing well against *The List*, Megan lies to him about working late to cover for her impromptu Thursday happy hour "date" with Drew. Peter is disappointed but quickly tries to reschedule for the weekend. Megan says she has to get back to him. She wants to leave things open so that Drew has a chance to ask her out the next day. Fair is fair, she figures.

Drew doesn't call on Friday. But he does e-mail her to say that he had an awesome time with her and he can't wait to see her when he gets back on Tuesday from his ski weekend. Funny, he hadn't even mentioned a ski trip. Megan wants to give him points, but she realizes that he hasn't even called her—even after they kissed! She feels that familiar antsy and disappointed "Colin feeling" once again. But part of her still feels hopeful as she replays all the nice things Drew said to her. Still, she feels kind of stupid that she kissed him. She calls Peter and tells him her weekend is "wide open."

Peter picks her up at her apartment on Saturday afternoon and gives her a pretty candle. "They had a craft show on the street near the hospital and I know that you like candles," he says. It isn't wrapped or anything but she thinks it is really sweet. She remembers picking up surprises for Colin here or there, but she can't remember the last time a man has surprised her with anything.

At lunch, Megan asks Peter about his week at the hospital. He doesn't say too much, only that it was hectic as usual and that a couple beers should cure him of the stress of the week. He listens intently about Megan's week at work. She describes a major Seinfeld moment when she forgot to hang up the other line during a customer conference call and inadvertently called the customer a liar, which ended up on the customer's voice mail. Peter laughs loudly and tells her not to worry about it, and says that if the boss does find out, she could just say that she was joking with the person in the next cube. Megan is so glad that he has taken her side. When she had told Drew the same story via e-mail, he told her what he would have done to proactively solve the problem with the customer. He also added "You've really got to watch that stuff."

Just like last weekend, she feels very at ease with Peter. After dinner they take a walk, get some ice cream, and talk some more. After a couple of blocks, Peter has finished his cone and they sit on a bench. He takes off his glasses, leans in, and says, "Megan, I can't take this anymore." She looks at him, surprised, as he leans in for a kiss. She nearly drops her hot fudge sundae. This is no ordinary kiss. This is a three-minute marathon kiss that is intense and sweet. After they unlock lips, Megan says "Um, wow. Yeah, wow." This man obviously is no amateur, and she immediately begins to see Peter as more than a nerdy, nice doctor. He is hot! They hold hands and walk back to Megan's apartment. They cuddle on the couch and spend the next three hours kissing, talking, and kissing some more. She feels like she's back in high school. She resists her urge to take it any further, and Peter, although very intense, remains "gentlemanly." They get Chinese takeout and rent a movie. When they finally say good night, Peter says "How about we catch some breakfast tomorrow, okay?" She agrees, and he is on his way. They spend the remainder of the weekend together. On Sunday night, he lets her know that he may not be able to call her until Wednesday because he's working an overnight shift at the hospital Monday night and has to prepare for grand rounds Tuesday night. Megan isn't worried because he's accounted for his time, and he sounds really sad that they have to part ways for a few days.

Peter surprises Megan with a call at work on Tuesday afternoon. He leaves a message on her voice mail to let her know how his day is going and asks if she wants to have dinner that night and hang out while he prepares his grand rounds. She's just about to call him back when her phone rings. It's Drew: "Hey, how are you?"

Megan is taken off guard and replies, "Uh, I'm fine. How about you?" Drew goes into his ski trip and this morning's meeting with his boss, and how it's almost quarter end and they aren't even halfway to their sales goal, and how he's going to get roasted if they don't "pick it up," and how half his reps are lazy and don't know what they're doing, and how he's going to have to fly to each of their territories to close deals for them in the next two weeks.

When he finally takes a breath, he says, "But I just wanted to let you know that I'm totally thinking about you and the great time we had last week. If you want, we could hang out after work tonight. This is the last time I'll have for a while." Megan thinks about their kiss and how she felt it in her toes and also about how funny and charming Drew is.

If this were the old pre-*List* Megan, she would have made every effort to see Drew again, just for the fun of it. But this is the new Megan, and she's sticking to *The List*. Peter has checked off every item with ease, while Drew has struggled to check off even one. She says, "You know Drew, I'm really used to guys calling me the day after they plant a kiss on me. The fact that you didn't call shows me that you're really not that interested. And the fact that of the last five minutes on the phone, you've spent four of them talking at me shows me that although you're good-looking, you're a big bore. Best of luck with your sales goals and your life. Goodbye."

It takes every bit of courage that she has to say it, but she smiles after she hangs up the phone. "Jackass," she says to herself out loud.

Drew looks at the receiver in stunned silence, "I can't believe she called me a jackass," he says to his work buddy.

Megan is so happy that during their last conversation Peter said she could page him at the hospital. She knows that means something. She calls Peter and tells him she'll be over that night. She is going to surprise him by bringing over homemade lasagna. In addition, she is going to stop at the bookstore and stock up on magazines so she won't bother him while he does his work. She can't wait to see his apartment. She can't wait to see him.

TARA

On Thursday morning, Tara feels a little down at work. Sure Patrick has checked off the *List* items thus far. He has called numerous times after their first date. In fact, he called Monday, Tuesday, and Wednesday nights. His last message said he would just wait for her to call, because he was beginning to feel like a huge ass. "Stalker is more like it," she thinks. She really doesn't know what to do. It's not like she has a ton of other people beating down her door.

She goes home around 6:00 P.M. and listens to the message on her answering machine: "Hey Tara, it's Bret. Hope you're well. I'm so sorry about missing last week's date. I want to make it up to you. I have to go to this black-tie event tomorrow night for the Architect's Institute and I'm wondering if you'd like to come with. It should be a really nice event. It starts at six-thirty. So . . . I'll give you a call later tonight. I've got a late school board meeting for a new high school we are working on. Uh . . . I should be done by nine o'clock or so. I'll give you a call from the road. Okay. Talk to you soon. Bye."

Tara's mind is spinning: black tie? This event will require a new dress—the red cocktail dress just won't do. If she leaves now she can make it to Saks in time to get a proper dress. She'll need shoes too. If she leaves work by 3:00 P.M. tomorrow she'll have time to get in for a manicure and pedicure.

She feels really nervous. She and Bret still have not met face to face. And this will certainly be an important first date. Even if it doesn't work out, she'll have a great time dressing up. She heads off to the mall and there she finds a perfect cream-colored sheath dress and Stuart Weitzman sandals. It is minimal and elegant but "less is more" when dating an architect.

Tara gets home promptly at 9:00 P.M., and sure enough, Bret has called. She sees his number on her Caller ID but he hasn't left a message. "Maybe he figures that I'll call him back," she thinks. She fishes his number off Caller ID and then sits there, frozen.

She hasn't even met this guy yet, and already she is feeling things that just aren't right at such a preliminary point in "the game." She decides to go through with it and call him. But, after about four rings, there is no answer. She leaves him a message: "Hi Bret, this is Tara. I'd love to go with you tomorrow. Um, maybe you could give me a call back tonight to confirm the details of where and how we can meet up. I'll be up late working on a project for work [she lies]. So . . . just give me a buzz. Otherwise, give me a call at work tomorrow. Talk to you soon." Midnight comes and Bret still hasn't called. Tara finally goes to sleep.

The next morning at work, she does not leave her desk for fear that she'll miss Bret's call. She even calls home and checks her machine just to make sure he hasn't confused her numbers. There is a message! It's just Patrick. "He who never quits," she thinks to herself.

She decides to scoot out of work to buy a new handbag to match her dress. She is sure that if she just stops watching the phone, it will ring.

When she gets back from her extra-long lunch at 1:30, Bret still has not called.

She decides to call Patrick. His message mentioned getting together over the weekend. She figures that it will be the most ideal situation if she could still spend time with Patrick during the early stages of her relationship with Bret. It will keep her busy and keep Bret on his toes. She and Patrick make plans to go out for lunch on Sunday.

Finally, at 3:30 P.M. the phone rings, and it's Bret: "Hey I'm so sorry we didn't connect last night. The school board meeting was canceled so I got home early, for once, and decided to go play soccer. I didn't want to wake you up. Are we on for tonight?"

Tara is dumbfounded. Did he not get her message telling him that she would be up late? "You know Bret, it's kind of late in the day to confirm plans," she says sharply.

There is silence. Finally, he says, "I'm sorry. I guess I dropped the ball again. But from what I hear about you, you are an experienced social butterfly. You can't be so cruel as to make an introverted dullard like me attend a fancy event alone?"

"I don't know. I just . . ." she replies.

"Come on. I'll make it up to you. How about a pre-party drink at the Meridian Club?"

That gets her attention. It is something like $15,000 a year for a mere junior membership at the club. She has never been there before.

"Okay. That sounds fun," she says in the most casual manner she can muster. He makes an extra effort to ask her when he can pick her up, where she lives, and the color of her dress.

They get off the phone and she grabs her keys and bolts out of her chair. She has to hustle home. When Bret picks her up, he looks amazing in his tux. He jokingly shakes her hand and says, "It's nice to meet you." He tells her she looks "stunning" and gives her a beautiful bouquet of white tulips. He opens the door to his Jaguar X Type. It is a short ride to the Club, so they don't have time to talk too much. They enjoy a martini in one of the front rooms. Bret is an excellent conversationalist. He asks her all about herself. He seems very interested in her job, her house, and her friends. She asks him questions too. He answers all of them very modestly and always makes sure to turn the conversation back to her. For the hundredth time, he tells her how glad he is to have finally met her.

At the event, Bret immediately starts introducing Tara to colleagues and clients.

As the night wears on she sticks by Bret's side, listening to his conversations and learning more about him. She learns that he is actually up for an award that night. Any other guy would have dropped that in somehow, but he hadn't. He is obviously very successful and likeable. People seem to gravitate toward him. Several of the wives Tara meets say things like, "Oh, Bret is just a doll. It's great to see him with a date." It gives her hope—maybe he never brought women to these things—perhaps he saw some potential with her? To cap off the evening, Bret wins his award. When a reporter from the local monthly magazine wants to take a photo of Bret with his award, Bret is quick to make sure Tara is included. She thinks, "Whatever went wrong with our communication over this night must have been a total fluke. Bret is every ounce the perfect gentleman."

When the evening ends, Bret thanks her for being his date and asks when he can see her again. Tara tells him she's free this weekend. "Well, great!" Bret replies. "I will give you a call and we'll do something. Oh, I almost forgot, LeBon, my favorite restaurant! Let me call them and see if they have reservations open, and I'll give you a call." He gives her a nice, polite kiss on the lips and they say good night at her doorstep.

As he drives away, Tara notices something shoved in her front door. It's a letter or card of some sort. She opens the envelope and finds a printout from a local pet shelter Web site—a picture of an adorable Jack Russell terrier. She had mentioned to Patrick that she was thinking of getting a Jack Russell. The card read: "Tara. Look who is waiting for you at the Humane Society! Call me, Patrick."

She will talk to him when she sees him on Sunday. Tonight, she is going to relive every moment of her dream date. She may even take a look at *The List* to read through the areas where she knows Bret has excelled. She is going to try hard to keep her options open, but she really wants to go out with Bret again.

CHRISTINE

Barry and Christine are far past the point of waiting for phone calls. They continue on in their blissful courtship. It is so nice to be relieved from the stress of "normal dating." For them, everything is simple.

WRAP-UP

To check off List Item 4, all dates should continue to be easy and fun with no pressure, no awkwardness, and no other people involved. It is still very early in courtship, and a List Man should still be trying to impress you—but more importantly, he should still only be interested in seeing you one-on-one. If your first date was "never-ending," you're ahead of the game. At this point in your budding relationship, a List Man:

☑ Keeps the momentum going by scheduling dates quickly and constantly.

☑ Is his own man, and he doesn't need his friends along for their opinion, their endorsement, or their assistance in pursuing or impressing you.

☑ Wants the intimacy that comes along with his being content with just you.

SEVEN

List

Item 5:

HE WANTS TO TALK TO YOU
EVERY DAY AND
WANTS TO SPEND ALL
HIS FREE TIME WITH YOU

Get comfortable, because this one is going to take some detailed explanation. Of the seven items on *The List*, this is the most important one.

By this point, you won't feel like you are "dating." You will feel something very easy and different. You will never wonder if the phone is going to ring because it will ring. You will never wonder when he is going to ask you out again because you will be in constant touch. You will never have to waste time overanalyzing his every move or asking your girlfriends, "What does it mean when he does this?" With a List Man, there will never be a doubt in your mind that he wants you—and wants you bad.

How do you know that he wants you? Because he gives you his time. Time is truly measurable. If a man won't give you his time, he isn't going to give you a ring. Everybody knows that when you get married, you are sharing your life. If a man wants to marry you, he will begin this "sharing" process during courtship. A List Man isn't pulling away after a few dates—he is pushing forward. You can't build momentum in a relationship without spending a ton of time together. And with the exception of things he has to do, he will clear away any optional activities so he can have more time to spend with you.

We all read the latest edition of *US Weekly* and sigh at the movie star who spells out "I love my girlfriend" in rose petals. But let's get serious: Bachelors are all about themselves. They love their stupid hobbies, boring friends, and "me" time. That's why the easiest and most accurate way to tell if you are "the one" for him is to see how much time he wants to spend with you.

Because a List Man is so happy being with you, he doesn't feel like he is giving up anything; he feels like he is gaining everything.

Being with you is the ultimate thrill. The season tickets to the minor league baseball team can wait (forever, hopefully). Friday nights with the boys are done (why would he spend time doing this when he has already met the woman of his dreams?), and the hours spent playing video games are on hold (though they may come back with a vengeance once you are married). A List Man isn't feeling shackled; he is feeling secure and happy. For the first time in his life, he is starting to realize that he may be ready for much, much more than just a girlfriend.

A List Man Has No Secrets

The List Man will gladly tell you what he is up to because he wants you to come along. If you can't come along, he'll still tell you what he is doing so you know he wishes that he didn't have to do it. If he has to go away on business, he will come back as soon as he can. He won't extend his trip to get some golf in or visit friends who live in the area. If a man doesn't account for his time, immediately and willingly, after a few dates, he is either hiding something or is not a List Man.

"Inseparable"

When describing their happy marriages, both parties use the word "inseparable" to describe their phenomenal courtships. That's why when you ask happily married people about how their courtships progressed, they will get a bit fuzzy. The key is that all of this happens quickly and is barely noticeable. It is the most natural thing in the world. If it takes months or years to get to the point where you are spending all of your time together (probably because you are living together), you are in trouble. As one woman explained:

> *"None of the other men I had dated in the past wanted to spend all of their free time with me. I was always wondering how they were feeling about me, and when they were going to call. It was exhausting and humiliating. When the right one came along, it was no effort at all. I knew how he felt about me. I didn't have to fret over a phone call because he was more often than not, right by my side."*

A List Man is smart. He realizes that he already spends forty or fifty or more hours a week away from you while he is working, so he doesn't want to be away from you more than that unless he has to be. Sure, he may have to make commitments from time to time (helping his sister move, driving his parents to the airport, attending an important event). But really, unless he is a world leader, his calendar is no more full or important than yours. Work is something he has to do, but anything else is thrown out the window for love. And while some people say, "That's unhealthy," we say, "Go, codependence!"

The truth of the matter is that happily married people are very codependent. They rely on each other completely. They call each other if they say something stupid at a meeting and want reassurance. They call each other to relate a funny thing that happened. They call to figure out what they are doing that evening.

When you're married, it is completely true that "two become one." A man who loves you wants you to depend on him. And you want him to depend on you. Of course he needs his own time (and so do you), but this is easy: He watches his show on television while you are

in bed reading decorating magazines. It might come in the form of a
night out with friends a few times a year. It might come in the form of
your going to the YMCA to work out while he stays home and works
in the yard or watches the kids. It is a little break here and there, not
an expectation or a necessity. A List Man loves to be around you

Knowing your List Man wants to be with you makes you feel
secure in your relationship. This will help you function well when you
have to be apart. After you are married, your life will return to a "new
normal." Mary's husband is gone for weeks at a time and was even
deployed for nine months. Sheila's husband sometimes works on
weekends and evenings. But with a firm foundation in place, this will
not faze a woman married to a List Man.

While healthy codependence is a part of a good marriage,
controlling behavior is not. The only thing a List Man can control is
how he spends *his* time—he won't try to control how you spend
your time. During courtship, he will make sure you know that he's
available whenever you want to see him. But he will never make you
feel uncomfortable or try to manipulate you when you can't see him.
A List Man would never make you feel smothered. If at any point you
feel nervous or scared by the pressure being applied, you will know
you are not with a List Man—you're with a control freak. This is not
normal behavior and you should end the relationship immediately.

What If He Doesn't Want to Spend All of His Time with You?

A man only interested in a girlfriend guards "his time" religiously. He
likes to set up a regular routine that keeps the woman somewhat
placated but also allows plenty of independent time for him. He

drops hints about loving how independent you are. He encourages you to go out with your friends as much as possible. He may be interested in being part of a couple, but he isn't interested in marriage.

Here's how it plays out. He decides after a few dates that he likes you enough to be exclusive. The adrenaline of the initial meeting and dates is enough to inspire him to make you his girlfriend. You start to spend part of the week together. He may stay at your place on Friday and Saturday nights. But he still requires and insists on his own time to clean his apartment, see his friends, exercise, work late, or pursue his hobbies. So, by Sunday afternoon he's ready to say goodbye for another few days. It's almost like a timer or a bell goes off. You have a great weekend together, and then you each go back into your corners. Because you're so desperate to be in a relationship and you don't want to risk scaring the guy away, you convince yourself that this is normal behavior. You think, "Well, we see each other all weekend long, and I'm definitely his girlfriend."

Kathy met a nice man through a personal ad, and they started dating. For the first few months of their relationship, he made it clear that he really preferred to see her on weekends. He lived in the city, and she lived in the suburbs, and they worked at opposite ends of town. It was just too inconvenient to try and see each other during the week. He said, "I just really like having the weekends to look forward to." He had to rev himself up to see her! During the week, he would work and live his own life. But come Friday night, he was ready to be a couple for the weekend. After a year or so, they did end up seeing each other during the week—and then all of the time. He had finally come on board. They got married and divorced within a year. Why?

Because Kathy didn't know what to do with herself when she wasn't trying to get more of his time. By the time she finally had it, she was bored and exhausted from the battle.

The moral of the story? From the get-go, a passionate List Man needs to see you all the time. This desire begins immediately—not months or years down the road. There is no such thing as inconvenience. He won't have to have breaks in between seeing you to have his own time or build up excitement to see you again. That is just silly.

Extra Credit Dating

Lots of men will actually spend an extra night with their girlfriend here or there and "count" this toward their weekly tally. This is what we call "extra credit dating." He figures that since he . . .

▷ Spent an extra night with you
▷ Surprised you by taking you to a movie during the middle of the day
▷ Took you on an expensive date
▷ Bought you jewelry
▷ Took you home to meet his family
▷ Spent a long weekend away with you
▷ Took a vacation with you

. . . He is now entitled to some extra time off from you later in the week, or should be able to go to Las Vegas with his friends, or should be able to sit home by himself and unwind alone.

Think about it. He tries to *earn* time away from you! He sees you as an obligation. With few exceptions, women want to spend all of their time with the man they love. There is nothing wrong with this. But here's the secret: If a man is in love with you, he will feel the same way. It is far better when a man spends every night sitting on the couch watching television with you than if he takes you on a weeklong cruise and needs his own time when you get back. You aren't a job. He isn't tracking how many hours or nights he spends with you and calculating what he can get in trade. Remember: he's not counting.

Yes, This Goes for Long-Distance Relationships, Too

Many women have met men on vacations, and after each returns to his or her respective reality, they keep hope alive by e-mailing and trying to figure out when they can see each other again. These e-crushes won't amount to anything. If a man wants to marry you, he will chase you to the ends of the earth.

Rachel lived in Australia when she met her future husband Rob at a party. He was born in Australia and was visiting relatives. He had lived and worked in the States for years. Regardless of the obstacles, Rob stated his intentions within a few weeks and they were officially engaged two months later and married within six months. Rachel moved to the United States after their wedding.

Rachel sounded Rob's Alarm, and he knew what he had to do. He could have used the distance as an excuse to carry on a relationship via e-mail. He could have said things like, "Well, if we lived in the same city, it would be a different story," and given Rachel the idea that if she moved to where he was, he would marry her. Or he could have spent months flying to visit her and asking her to visit him too. Instead, he knew that if he wasted time, he would risk losing her to another man. He did all the things on *The List* and came to the point where he wanted to spend all of his free time with Rachel—but she was half a world away. He couldn't go on like that. He proposed ASAP. They planned a fast wedding because their priority was to be together, not to spend a year planning a royal event.

Long-distance relationships offer a compelling reason for a man to act. Because of this, he will probably propose faster than a man who lives in the same town. It's really not that complicated. Whether you meet a man who lives 50 or 1,500 miles away, somebody is going to have to move. And you can't move without a ring on your finger. In many ways, a long-distance relationship is very easy to resolve.

False Alarm!

By now, you are done with your first few dates and need to do a serious check to make sure that he is really serious about marrying you. You'll be able to tell if The Alarm is ringing by tallying the amount of time he spends with you. Complete this thought:

Since we met, I have seen him ___ hours. When he's not at work he's with me. When he's not with me, he's _____.

If you are with a List Man, you should be able to complete this statement with ease because when he's not at work or with you, he voluntarily accounts for what he is doing (and if he's not at work or with you, he is sleeping or only doing things he has to do). You don't have to nag him about his whereabouts because he happily volunteers the information. You don't have to suggest you spend extra time together—he does.

If you can't complete this statement, or you can complete it but realize that he isn't spending his free time with you, then you aren't "the one." Sure, he approached you, called you, took you out, called you, and now wants to be your boyfriend. But he still wants his own time. You are feeling the ecstasy of easiness wearing off. You are starting to "work" for the relationship. Unfortunately, you are both the victims of a False Alarm. He may have felt very, very taken with you, but The Alarm never rang.

When a man holds back his time—or takes back his time little by little after dating you for months—he is not going to marry you. You have only invested a few weeks or a month in him, so it is best to cut your losses and move on.

Brenda met a man with great promise at a bar a few days before Christmas. He approached her, called right away (even on Christmas Day!), and said all the right things. After a few weeks of steady dating, he spent the night at her house. Early the next morning, as if he were on autopilot, he woke up and got dressed. "I have to go home to go running," he said. She was completely perplexed. After all, there were roads in her neighborhood too. Brenda had *The List* and knew this wasn't a good sign. Everything had been going well, and he seemed to be a great prospect. When he called her after his run, she gave him the cold shoulder. He defended his action by saying, "If I don't have my time to run, I'm not myself. I have to run." Right then and there she realized that she wasn't "the one." If he didn't want to spend his time with her after spending the night together, what would things look like in another six months? What man would rather go for a run than snuggle with his girlfriend?

As they talked, it came out that this really wasn't about the run. He told her that it seemed like she wanted more than he did. He said that things were moving too fast and that he didn't know if he wanted a serious relationship. Brenda said, "That's fine. I understand. Just don't contact me anymore." He e-mailed her a week later. She replied: "Bob, you told me that you weren't interested in a serious relationship with me. When I said don't contact me, I meant it." Three months later—out of the blue—he tried to call her several times. She watched his name show up on her Caller ID. By that time, she had met a man who wanted to spend all of his time with her. (PS: She and her List Man got engaged that June.)

Please don't make the mistake of thinking you can change his need for "away time." If you do, you will become one of those women who is happy when she is with her boyfriend and sad when they are apart. Don't think that you are too needy and convince yourself that you need to have your own life. If you wanted your "own life," you wouldn't be interested in getting married, would you? Men like women who have their "own lives" because it gives them more time to themselves. But it shouldn't be this difficult, and it shouldn't be a game. It is best to drop him and find a List Man. Here's what you say:

> *"Listen, _____, this just isn't what I'm looking for. We still have our separate lives for the most part. I have had boyfriends before, and I'm just ready for more than that now."*

You don't need to get into the time thing. He will debate you until he is blue in the face. When he challenges you or says that he is serious about you, just say:

"I just feel in my gut that this isn't where I need to be right now. I can't really explain it, but I want to find a man who is madly in love with me. When that happens, I'll know it. And it just isn't happening with you."

End of story. It is hard to part ways, but you are doing the right thing. You can't waste time on a man who isn't going to marry you. And your reward will come soon enough because when you are with a List Man, you'll never part ways. Ashley explains:

"We were inseparable after about one month. I was struck by his unashamed interest and lack of game playing. I never had to wonder if he was attracted to me, and I never sensed that he was 'playing hard to get.' After a few weeks, he surprised me by waiting at my car after work with a rose in hand. That was where we had our first kiss, and he told me that he wasn't seeing anyone else, and that he wanted things to go to the next level. We lived across town from each other, and sometimes we would only be able to see each other for thirty minutes. We eventually just never wanted to leave each other after dates and church, and would stay as long as we could without making complete zombies out of each other the next day at work."

A List Man Doesn't Take Additional Responsibilities When He Is Courting You

It logically follows that because he wants to spend all of his time with you, he isn't looking to take on any more obligations. Whatever commitments he had when he met you are enough for him. During the crucial, passion-filled, early stages of dating, he is focused on you and doesn't want to take on anything new.

For some non–List Men, it isn't enough to have their "negotiated" time away from their relationship. After months or years, they want to have even more time to themselves. Melissa's long-term boyfriend decided to start coaching a kid's soccer team on Saturdays. This was a major hindrance to the relationship. Not only did it take Sean away on Saturdays, but Friday evenings were also taken while he prepared for the game and then turned in early. Melissa was left on her own to go out with girlfriends or watch television alone in her apartment. This worked well for Sean because since the beginning of their relationship, he had never enjoyed spending Friday nights or Saturdays with Melissa. He wanted this time to "wind down" from his work week in whatever way suited him that particular week. His shift to being a couple always began on Saturday night.

This meant that Melissa was yet another obligation he needed to schedule. When Melissa heard about the team (after the decision was made—he never asked her for her opinion, of course), she expressed her disappointment that he was making this commitment. After two years of dating, she still did not see him as much as she wanted to. His defense was to make her feel needy and unsupportive because coaching the team was a favor to his boss. He assured her that this was an honor and would help him get ahead at work, and he reminded her that it was only for eight weeks.

When his commitment was up, he decided to volunteer again for the next season. For a while, Melissa still spent Friday nights at home alone or with her single girlfriends. She tried to convince herself that it was enough to spend the rest of the weekend with Sean. It's a good thing Melissa eventually followed *The List* and broke up with Sean. (PS: Within two months of breaking up with Sean, several men had asked Melissa for dates. She feels confident that a List Man is coming her way.)

Work Jerk

The most common strategy men use to get away from their girlfriends is to hide behind work. Sometimes they even have the nerve to try to garner sympathy! Think about it. He would rather be at work than with you. Does it get any worse than that? Do not buy *any* excuses relating to work that relate to *not* seeing you. It doesn't matter if he's trying to get ahead in a new job, finishing his master's degree, starting or running his own business. It does not matter!

A List Man is as steady at work as he is at courtship. If he were asked to take on a special project, he would do one of these two things:

1. Bow out gracefully because at the present moment he is focused on you. He gets the fact that in the work world, one is asked over and over again to take on extracurricular responsibilities. He knows that it is okay to say no.

2. If he *had* to take on an extra workload, he would explain the
   situation to you. He would say how much he hates it, tell you
   how long the obligation will last, and make every attempt to
   be with you regardless of the obstacles. For example, if Sean
   were a List Man, Melissa would be invited to stay at his place
   on Friday nights. If he hadn't prepared for his game during
   his lunch hour, he would do it as quickly as he could. She
   would be welcome to help him or just hang out and watch
   television. The only time Sean would be away would be the
   two hours on Saturday morning.

If you decide to overlook a man who doesn't spend time with
you because he has to work, be warned that if you do get married,
you may spend many weekday nights or weekend afternoons alone.
There are two types of men at work:

▷ The man who dawdles at the office, is always up to happy
   hour with co-workers, and can't wait for out of town business
   trips to get away from his wife and kids.
▷ The type who works his butt off so he can get home ASAP
   and doesn't stay out of town any longer than he has to.

Which kind of man do you want to end up with? We are all for hard-
working men, but a List Man knows that it's much better to pursue
major career-advancement opportunities after you're engaged or
married. There are several good reasons for this:

▷ He will have secured you and made sure that you aren't

wooed away by a man with more free time to spend with you.

▷ Any improvements he makes to his resume will directly benefit both of you.

▷ He knows that you are happy and content with your commitment and will have your own positive extracurricular things to focus on, such as planning your wedding, setting up a home, or raising kids.

Society pressures women into thinking men won't like them if they are needy. That's simply not true. The man that you are meant to be with loves to be with you all the time and is glad that you feel the same way. He would never encourage you to spend more time away from him. He is okay with it when you want to do your own thing, but he doesn't make you feel like a dope because you want to be with him all the time. He thinks that is just fine.

LIFE IN LISTOPIA

MEGAN

Now that Drew is completely out of the picture, Megan focuses her attention on Peter. She is all set to go to his apartment and hang out while he prepares his grand rounds. She can't believe how comfortable she feels. She remembers how Colin would frequently work late in the office even though he had everything he needed to work from home. "I'll get more done here," he would tell her. If she had to work at home on an evening or weekend, Colin would always take the opportunity to leave the house and be by himself or with his friends.

She packs up the lasagna and stops by the store to buy a stack of magazines to keep her occupied and out of his way. She buys the usual tabloids and fashion magazines. She also picks up a copy of *Chic Bride* magazine. A good friend of hers has just gotten engaged and she is putting together a little gift basket. She loves looking at the bouquets and floral arrangements and daydreaming about the works of art that she would create in her own little floral shop. Lastly, she buys a copy of *Serious Gamer* magazine for Peter as a reward for finishing his work. It kind of bugs her that he's so crazy about video games, but she figures that she would rather have a man who does his hobbies at home than out on the town.

Since her relationship with Colin ended, she has done a lot of soul searching. She realized that she is a lonely person in a way and wants a spouse who actually wants to be around her all the time. A year ago, she would have thought this was a major weakness. But since meeting Peter and reading *The List*, she realizes that this is not only okay, it's perfectly normal.

When she arrives at Peter's place, they have a nice dinner together, he compliments her cooking over and over and he finally says that he has to get to work. "Should I go to the other room?" Megan asks.

"Only if you want to watch the tube. Otherwise, you can hang here. I think I can resist you!" Peter smiles. They spend the next few hours in contented silence. Megan devours her gossip rags, even cross-referencing her *In Touch* with her *US Weekly* to make sure she's got the latest secret celeb wedding news straight.

When Peter is finally done preparing his presentation, Megan offers to act as audience. Peter laughs and says, "It's not like the business world where I have to be real polished. It's all just boring facts about a boring medical case." But he walks her through some of it, and she is impressed. She can tell that he is ready to be done with work. It's late and he asks if she wants to stay the night or if he should drive her home: "I want you to stay but if you want to go home, I can take you." (This contrasts with Colin's usual, something like, "Well, it's really late, we probably both need to get a good night's sleep.") She can tell he would be happy if she stayed. And he had to have noticed that she has brought her "shack-bag." (In the early days with Colin, she shacked up a lot. But after a few weeks, she felt like she was limited to two or three nights a week.)

She says, "I'll stay." It isn't a big deal for either of them. There is a little smooching, but they are both tired, so they soon say good night. Megan feels very happy and content.

The next day, Peter drops her off at work and says he'll call her after he's done for the day and they can catch dinner. This routine goes on for several weeks. They see each other almost every day. When Peter is not working, he is with her. On one of the weekends he has to go to a "residents' retreat" at a lodge not too far outside of the city. He says it's an annual thing and that he can't get out of it. She knows he doesn't want to go and tries to tell him that it will be fun. She is happy to know that he would rather be with her than anywhere else.

It's funny. Even after dating for a year, Megan only saw Colin a few nights a week at most. There was always—what seemed at the time—a logical reason for this. He had to work late, or he had plans with his friends, or he needed to do laundry, and so on. Colin would always present it in such a nice way: "I've got to run some errands and you should go home and rest—you worked hard this week." Now, Megan can see that Colin really felt he needed his space away from her. Sometimes, she would call his apartment on nights when he was home "doing laundry," and he wouldn't answer his phone. She suspected that he just didn't want to talk. She would drill him about it the next day and he would just say, "Oh, I must have been in the laundry room. I didn't check messages." Or, he would leave his cell behind or not have it charged. What a fool she was.

That is not the case with Peter. They call each other constantly. It is hard to believe that a busy doctor is more reachable than a junior account executive was!

Because Peter and Megan are totally inseparable, when he leaves for the weekend apart, she feels very secure. Lonely—but secure. She decides to go out with some girlfriends for drinks. They have a good time, and Megan is approached by no fewer than three men at the various bars. She flirts politely. One even asks for her phone number. She gives him her business card just to show her friends from an experiment *The List*. Sure enough, he does contact her . . . via e-mail, five days later, just to chat. She laughs. It confirms how lucky she is to have found Peter.

Peter calls her on Sunday night when he returns from the retreat and asks if she wants to come over. It feels so good to be wanted and needed by Peter. She goes over to his place and asks all about the retreat. Peter says it was fun, but that he really couldn't stop thinking about her.

She stays over at Peter's that night. But she can't sleep—her mind is on overdrive. She is sure that Peter is definitely "the one." But does he feel the same way? She is pretty sure that he does. But still, there are two List items left. It is hard to picture even-headed, practical Peter making a fast proposal.

Although Megan thinks he is asleep, Peter is also staring into the darkness. When he was tidying up for Megan's arrival, he found something interesting under his couch: *Chic Bride* magazine.

TARA

Tara's phone rings on Saturday. She feels disappointed that the call isn't from Bret. It's her friend Kim, checking up on her date with Bret. She wants to see if Tara feels like grabbing a cup of coffee. Tara says she has to meet Patrick for lunch but that coffee sounds great. At the coffee shop, Kim starts to talk about her dating life. She is Tara's age and is also looking to get married soon. She says she has been out on three blind dates in the last two months, all of which resulted in nothing. Two of the men never even called her, and the one who did had very recently been divorced, which left her wary.

Tara resists the urge to brag about her blind date with Bret. She tells Kim not to give up hope. Tara also suggests that Kim try online dating. She tells her about Patrick and that even though he's not really her type, he is still a nice guy. She looks at her watch and realizes it is time to make her way to the café to meet Patrick for lunch. She tells Kim, "Hey, you can meet him if you want. I'm meeting him at Vinny's Grill in fifteen minutes."

Kim walks with her. Outside the restaurant, Tara quickly introduces Kim to Patrick. Kim is a little slow to leave but Patrick moves things along by saying, "I think the hostess just called our name." Over lunch, Patrick asks if Tara received his Jack Russell card. Tara thanks him for the thought. She says that she's not ready for a pet yet and doesn't want to go to the Humane Society until she's ready to adopt. Just then, she hears her cell phone ringing. What if it's Bret?

She tells Patrick that she has a call from work that she has to take and that she will be right back. She gets out of her seat in time to hear the voice mail beeping on her phone. Bret has left a message: "Hey Tara, just wanted to say what a splendid evening I had last night. You were a definite hit. So many of my friends approached me to tell me how much they liked you. Anyway, I'm out running errands today and probably won't be home until after six. Just wanted to see if you had plans for dinner. I'm a bit over the formal thing, so maybe we could just catch some sushi over by my house. Let me know." He didn't leave her his number, but it's on the Caller ID. She takes a deep breath and decides to try his cell back. No answer. Then she tries his home phone. He picks up, out of breath.

"Oh, hey Tara. What's going on?" he asks as if he hadn't just called her and asked her out!

"Well, I got your message and that sounds great."

He insists on picking her up. What a guy! She rushes through the rest of her date with Patrick and says she has some errands to run, so he doesn't offer to walk her home. At home, she straightens things up and starts her beauty countdown. She bathes, primps, and picks the perfect casual sundress. Her phone rings and it is Kim. She asks how lunch went. Tara says that it was okay but that Patrick just isn't "the one" for her. Kim quickly says, "Well, I don't want to be pushy, but I thought he was really cute. We have to look out for each other!" Tara is taken aback. She doesn't want Patrick for herself, but she isn't sure if she is ready to completely let him go. He is a good friend, and his attention is flattering. But Kim has set her up in the past and she couldn't really say no. Besides, she figures that Patrick hasn't approached Kim in the first place so it was unlikely that a List relationship would result. She tells Kim to "go for it" and gives her Patrick's number.

Bret comes in and, since they had been so rushed for their first date, he asks for a tour. She has made sure everything is perfect. He gushes over her 1920s house and all of the architectural details. He tells her how perfect her decorating is and how he could really use her help with his new place. Imagine that—an architect asking for her help!

When they finish the tour, she pours him a glass of wine and he gives her a quick kiss on the lips. They review last night's event and she asks him for details on his award. He kisses her again. The phone rings. She just lets it ring. Patrick leaves a message and they can hear it on the machine: "Hey darlin' . . . Listen, your friend Kim just called me. Uh, she said that you gave her my number. So, uh, listen. I get it. You aren't interested and that's fine. I thought maybe I could, uh, convince you. But hey! I gave it my best effort but even a silly guy like me gets a bit tired of playing the fool. So, I'll quit calling and maybe I'll see you around. Take care."

She just stares at Bret. In a way, the moment is perfect. Here is another man she rejected, leaving her a message while another man listened. He smiles at her and says, "Well, I guess I'm the lucky guy."

In Bret's car, she feels a little bad. Patrick's message is on her mind. He sounded like he was trying hard to make light of the situation. But still, she knows what it feels like to be on the other end of things. She is just relieved that it is over.

She certainly recognizes Patrick's good qualities. And he would have made a great friend, but she simply can't deny the flutter in her heart that she felt when she heard Bret's message. Even *The List* says that you can't make chemistry happen. It just is. And she gave him a fair chance, didn't she? It was that wonderful early love feeling that she just couldn't seem to muster when she thought about Patrick. Sure he was a good kisser, and he was very funny and easy to be around—but when it came down to it, the spark is so much stronger with Bret. She has to follow her heart.

And she is so glad that she did. They have an amazing evening. Bret is so handsome and interesting; she loves being with him. A couple of his friends are also at the restaurant with their girlfriends and Bret invites them over to meet Tara and drink sake. Tara is a little bugged because she would rather have a romantic evening. And she knows what *The List* says about one-on-one time. But what was he supposed to do? His friends were sitting right there! It would have been rude to not include them. Besides, she has a fabulous time as the center of attention and gets along great with all of his friends. It is always so much fun to meet new people and these people are all well-dressed, interesting, and wickedly funny.

It is another perfect date. Afterward he asks her if she'd like to stop by his place for coffee. Tara doesn't hesitate and almost as soon as they close the front door, they are all over each other. She immediately sobers up and enjoys every moment of their passionate embracing. Soon, they are in bed and there is no stopping what has started.

The next morning, Bret looks adorable in his college sweatshirt and running shorts. He says he's going to step out to get some bagels and coffee. Tara is in heaven. He is gorgeous and she is definitely in love. Now, she has to gather her wits about her and play the game. She's not going to screw this one up.

Meanwhile, poor Patrick is licking his wounds. He feels bad. Tara could have at least had the class to tell him that Kim would be calling. He was totally taken off guard by her message. "To hell with Tara," he thinks to himself. He is a nice guy and he knows it. He didn't deserve to be treated poorly by Tara. But because he is a good guy, Patrick makes up his mind that very moment to forgive Tara and move on. He replays Kim's message. She has such a sweet voice. And the way she got through the awkwardness of the phone call made him smile. "I have never done this before, but . . ." When he remembers how cute and bubbly Kim was, he is pretty sure that she has never called a man before.

He decides to call her. "Hey, of course I remember you! I am so flattered that you called me. And to reward you for your bravery, I'm going to bring you the best bagel and coffee you have ever had." For Kim, the List Man cometh!

CHRISTINE

Barry and Christine have been inseparable over the last few weeks. They talk to each other every day, usually two or three times a day, and spend every night and weekend together. They have already discussed rings. Christine has dreamed of a yellow diamond, and although it is way out of Barry's budget, he wants to buy it for her. He tells her that he may cash out some of his stocks. (Barry is a savvy, but conservative, investor.) But he makes it clear that she should not think one more minute about it because she will have her ring very soon. They decide to make arrangements to meet each other's families. Christine invites her parents over for dinner, and Barry makes plans to take Christine to his parents' lake place to meet his entire family over the next holiday weekend, two weeks away.

WRAP-UP

Time is measurable and a sure indicator of what you mean to him. After all, if he won't share his time, he certainly isn't prepared to share his heart and his life with you. Things to remember about this most important item on *The List*:

☑ If a man is going to marry you, he wants to be with you all the time. No excuses.

☑ After a few weeks, you will no longer be "dating"—you will be inseparable.

☑ He will still works hard at his job, but he won't take on extra responsibilities to get away from you.

☑ If a man doesn't want to spend all of his free time with you, it means there has been a False Alarm. It is hard to believe after getting this far on *The List* that things aren't going to work out. But if he won't give you his time, he won't give you a ring.

EIGHT

List

Item 6:

HE DEMONSTRATES
UNCONDITIONAL
LOYALTY

Your man has passed the first five items on *The List* with flying colors, and things are getting much more serious. You've already gauged his feelings based on how much time you spend together. Now you have another litmus test to introduce: Is he loyal to you? Does he always have your back? If he is a List Man, he will take your side on matters of importance because he sees you as an extension of himself. During the early phases of dating, this is hard to measure, but it can be done.

A List Man Won't Criticize You While He Is Courting You

You know already that if you are the one, he will love you "as is." All of the things that you have tried to change about yourself in the past because you thought they were turnoffs are fine with him. Sure, you will eventually get on his nerves from time to time. And he may even think to himself, "Man, she's crazy." But he accepts the whole package and knows that your good points far outweigh your not-so-good points.

Of course, once you have sealed the deal with him, he will slip up from time to time. After Jon proposed to Mary, he left to do army business for a month. She remembers very clearly that her wonderful man, the one who had been so understanding about her debt load, was suddenly very judgmental and unsympathetic when she spoke of her credit card balance. These types of occurrences are just part of relationship reality. But a man who criticizes a woman *before* the deal is closed is not worth waiting for. Don't try to convince yourself that he is looking out for you. Until he has really made a commitment, he doesn't have the right to criticize you about anything. That includes your drinking, smoking, eating, or shopping habits.

A List Man Won't Cheat or Lie

It goes without saying that a List Man will never lie to you about any matter of importance. He will—and should—lie to you about trivial matters. When you ask him if he likes your new short haircut, he should respond with an enthusiastic "Yes!" Or, if you said something dumb to a coworker, he should listen to your concerns but not add to them. A List Man will never sneak around or deceive you in any way.

You Are the Only Woman in a List Man's Life

Another key to assessing a man's loyalty is to observe how he deals with women from his past. A List Man will not keep anybody in his life if it makes you uncomfortable. A List Man knows that you are the one and will distance himself from any women who send out the wrong signal. Whether she is an overfriendly ex, a flirtatious friend, or a coworker he's dated a few times, a List Man will make it clear that he is unavailable.

Janelle had only been dating Philip for two weeks when she found out that he had plans to go on a ski trip. He was going alone, and she thought this was strange. Also, he seemed very uncomfortable talking to her about it. When she pressed him for details, he confessed that he might run into a woman from his past on the trip. Then it came out that he had planned the trip months in advance and part of the plan was to stay with this woman. Even though he had just started seeing Janelle, he told her that he didn't want to put their relationship in jeopardy. Well, of course she told him that since it was so early in the relationship, he could do whatever he wanted. But, she added, if he did go on the trip, she couldn't see him anymore. He canceled the trip. He lost a lot of money in deposits and tickets, but he did it anyway.

You can play it as cool as you want and convince yourself that after a week of being together he doesn't owe you anything. That's wrong. If he thinks that you are "the one," he owes you everything.

He Will Support You No Matter What

The man in your life isn't your girlfriend. He probably won't be able to talk for hours on end about what your she-troll boss did to you at work. But when you tell him what is going on, he will say something like, "She's really out of line." He won't say something like, "Well, you probably shouldn't have said that," or, "You know how you get sometimes." Is there anything worse than having to defend yourself to somebody who should be in your corner?

When Jackie was out for dinner with her long-term boyfriend and his friends, she made a joke that could have seemed offensive, but certainly wasn't to her audience. Everybody at the table laughed, but her boyfriend piped in with, "Hey, I don't like that." He made her look like a fool in front of his friends. If he were a List Man, he would have just laughed at her joke and forgotten about it.

Over the course of your marriage, you will say and do many things that make waves. And sometimes, you will regret these things. But you don't want your husband to say things like, "You need to apologize for saying that," or, "What was going through your head?" He needs to understand that you are perfectly able of kicking yourself, thank you very much. He may think to himself, "Boy, what was she thinking," but to you he will say, "Well, I don't think it's a big deal. You'll figure out how to make it right if you think that's what needs to happen."

Every woman wants to feel protected, and a man provides this protection by defending you whenever you need him to.

It won't matter if you quit every job you have after six months because your boss always seems to be a loser. It won't matter if you always have your foot in your mouth in front of people. He knows that this is the way you are and accepts it.

And—by the way—you should behave the same way toward him. It is so easy to cringe at something he did at work and tell him what a bad idea this or that was. It's tempting to put him down in front of your friends so you look cool. But how mean is this? If you aren't on his side all the time, he won't share the challenges of his life with you, and you will end up shut out.

A List Man Doesn't Care What Others Think about Your Relationship

When you have a Fairy Tale courtship, you will find out who your friends are and so will he. Some people don't know about, or believe in, the concept of "I saw her, I was ready, and that was it." Because it hasn't happened to them, they may have a hard time supporting your relationship.

Norm, who proposed to Deborah in a matter of weeks, shares this story:

"The decision was quick and took Deborah by surprise. A thing I always scoffed at in the movies—who in their right mind is actually

surprised? I don't believe that it was rash. We had both been married before and knew what we wanted and did not want in a partner. Our temperament, educational background, and future hopes and goals were similar, and this solidified our feelings and trust. Because of the lightning speed that we moved at, we knew we would face uncertainty from family and friends. But from my end, any negative reactions to my quick proposal were no match to the certainty of my happiness while in the company of Deborah."

If your happily married friends are apprehensive, cut them some slack. After all, they have watched you make mistakes before. They wonder if you are a good judge of husband character. They may not know about *The List* or may not understand how it has helped you get to this point. Because you have only been dating this guy for fewer than thirty days, your friends will be extra worried that things are moving too fast. They don't want to see your heart broken—again. But they do want you to be happy and so they'll come around soon enough. It is likely that when they meet your List Man, they will understand why you are so certain about him. You know who is on your side in life, but you also have to understand that not everybody is on your time line. Your happily married friends, family, and supportive single friends will soon share your enthusiasm. They will be eagerly awaiting your engagement and will be very excited to help you plan your wedding.

Some of your single girlfriends or unhappily married friends will be much slower to warm up to your new relationship. They may be jealous. They may be sad that they are losing a fellow single to hang out with. They will miss your tales of dating hell and the opportunity to pity you or advise you. Try not to worry about this either. Just politely ignore them. If they are your friends, they will come around by the time the wedding invitations are in the mail. If they don't come around and support your relationship, you can fire them when you have time. Most likely, they will just go away on their own.

The List Man and his friends and family will also have some decisions to make. With any luck, because he is such an upstanding person, he will have great friends and family. They will be delighted. But don't be surprised if he has some "less than thrilled" people to deal with. They will be experiencing the same emotions as your friends and family. Odds are that you will dwell on this much more than he does. It will irritate you to no end that his friends are badmouthing your relationship. It will get on your last nerve if his sister or mother is nice to your face but talks behind your back. You will wonder if he really loves you because he won't seem that concerned.

Here's what will happen with a List Man: He will eventually distance himself from anybody who doesn't support your relationship. First, he will try to ease your fears and make light of the situation. He will say things like "Yeah, _____ can be like that" or "_____ probably didn't mean it that way." But his radar is on, and he knows that the situation isn't great.

That's why you probably don't need to nag him about it. He isn't going to make a big *Melrose Place* scene and fire somebody the way you wish he would, but he will just make a mental note not to invest any more in the friendship. Or, in the case of his family members, he will just wait it out, knowing that if they don't come on board, his relationship with them will become strained. Because he prefers one-on-one dates and wants to spend all his free time with you, there may not be an issue at all.

If somebody is really stressing you out and trying to come between you and your List Man, ask him to set that person straight. If he is truly a List Man, he will do it. Let him handle it in his own way and try not to bug him about it or criticize how he managed things.

Both of you need to focus on each other and not let outsiders spoil your courtship. Because you have been in your cocoon and haven't spent much time with other people, you need not worry about having people's approval. If, after you are engaged, people are still rude or disapproving—it's time for him (and you) to give them a pink slip. And if he doesn't, you need to reconsider where things are between you.

When Angie was in the midst of a very fast-moving courtship with Dan, her soon-to-be fiancé wanted to bring her to brunch to meet his two best buddies. Dan preferred one-on-one dates, but his friends were making him feel guilty for not being available. The whole event was very awkward. Dan's friends were cold and sarcastic to Angie. She tried her best to impress them, but when they responded so poorly, she figured "To hell with it." She bit her tongue during the meal but let Dan have it once they were out of the restaurant. Like most List Men, Dan really liked his friends, but his relationship with them had always centered on going places to meet women. Now that Dan had Angie, he saw that he didn't have all that much in common with his friends. He was so focused on being in love that he stopped calling his friends, and they didn't call him either.

One day, Angie walked into the local coffee shop and saw one of the friends sitting and reading a newspaper. He pretended not to see her and actually left the restaurant rather than talk to her! Of course she reported this back to Dan, but he had already figured out that it was a waste of time and energy to try to have a relationship with people who weren't on the same page. Eventually, that same guy did resurface (once he was dating a woman he liked), and Angie and Dan were happy to see him occasionally.

Sometimes a man will refuse to nip these issues in the bud. Rather than be the "bad guy" to his friends or family members, he would prefer to pretend the situation doesn't exist. He figures that eventually you will stop nagging him about it. But his inaction causes you to lose respect for him. You rightfully question his devotion and loyalty. If the man you have been dating has gotten this far on *The List*, it is doubtful that he would put you in this spot. But if he does, you need to reassess.

LIFE IN LISTOPIA

MEGAN

When Peter finds the bridal magazine that Megan left, he is actually a little relieved. He knows that he loves Megan and that he feels something for her he has never felt before. He is happy to know that marriage is on her mind too.

One evening Megan and Peter are eating pizza at his apartment when his phone rings. Megan hears Peter: "Hey . . . I'm fine. This weekend? No, I'm not working. That sounds great. You can meet Megan. Okay, great we'll see you then." He comes back in the room, "That was my sister. She's coming into town on Friday with her husband and baby. They want to stay here." Megan replies, "Oh, that's cool. Well, you don't have to worry about me, I have a bridal shower to go to and I'm sure I can find something to occupy my time." Peter says that he wants her to meet them and asks if she can get together for dinner on Friday night. "Sure," says Megan. She smiles to herself. Colin didn't introduce her to any members of his family for six months—and even then it was only because she guilt-tripped him into it.

The week passes, and by Friday night Megan is anxious to meet Peter's sister. She knows that his sister's name is Tiffany, that she's five years younger and his only sibling. She doesn't work and had her baby at twenty-four. Megan has seen a picture of Peter with his sister taken at Tiffany's house one Christmas, and Megan noticed there were a ton of knick-knacks in the background: dolls, Hummels, and a lot of stuff that looked like it was from The Franklin Mint. Megan's a little worried about finding things in common; after all, she is certain it will be important to have Tiffany's approval. After work, Megan decides to pick up a little gift to break the ice.

When she arrives at the restaurant, Peter is watching for her. He waves to her and she heads over to the table. He stands up and puts his arm around her when she arrives. His sister is blond and petite, her husband is a big guy with a crew cut, and their baby is covered with mushed cookie and is starting to scream loudly. Megan quickly puts her hand out and says, "It's so nice to meet all of you! My gosh, he is just adorable!" Everybody is fussing with the baby and nobody responds. She quickly looks into her purse and pulls out a snow globe of the city. "I wanted to get you a little token of your trip." Tiffany smiles and thanks her. Peter smiles at her and tells her to have a seat. He introduces Megan in a way that makes her know that he has mentioned her to his family before: "Well, this is

Megan!" She notices that his sister doesn't say anything to help her feel comfortable.

Most of the conversation is focused on Oklahoma and family and friends back home. Peter tries to steer the conversation to Megan, but Tiffany and Jared show no interest, so it's back to the triumphs of the college football team and the latest on the new mall going up back home.

Megan sits politely and occasionally interjects just to show some interest in the conversation. It feels like such an effort. She is bored, and very tired from a long day at work. Peter squeezes her knee under the table. When they finally leave, Peter pulls her aside and gives her a quick kiss. He thanks her for coming and apologizes if the conversation was a bit lacking: "They just don't get around much." He tells her that he wishes she could stay over tonight, but Megan cuts him off. "With a baby at your place? No, that would not be appropriate. Besides, I'm exhausted." Peter says he'll call her tomorrow and they part.

Megan thinks a lot about how little she has in common with Tiffany. Peter seems pretty normal; he fits into the city life well. It is amazing that Tiffany is his sister. Megan immediately starts thinking about going back to Oklahoma some day to meet the rest of his family. What will his parents be like? She knows that his mom is a retired schoolteacher who enjoys knitting (from the number of afghans around Peter's apartment) and his father is a CPA who likes hunting and fishing. Megan's family is a crazy bunch of city-raised Irish Catholics who love to eat, play cards, and debate politics. Only the strong survive in her family, and someone like Tiffany would be eaten for lunch. She loves her family, but now she is just as worried about Peter meeting them. Oh, well, she is getting too far ahead of herself. She thinks about *The List*. Peter has demonstrated kindness over and over again, but loyalty? Hmm.

Meanwhile, back at Peter's place his sister puts baby Harrison to bed and her husband turns in too. Tiffany sits with Peter on the sofa and says, "Megan seems nice."

Peter replies, "She is, she's a great girl; I've really never felt this way about someone before. I think this it's the real deal."

"Did you know that Summer got a divorce?" Tiffany asks Peter. Summer was Peter's college girlfriend.

"That's too bad," he replies, hoping she will change the subject.

"Well, we had lunch the other day and she asked about you."

Peter doesn't respond.

"Well, I thought you two were great together. She doesn't have any kids or baggage and she looks amazing."

Peter cuts her off, "Okay Tiff, I see where this is going. But you have to realize that we broke up years ago. And we broke up for a reason. Let's just drop it, okay?"

With that Tiffany gets up to go to bed. "Okay, I just told Summer that I would mention it when I was up here. Forget I brought it up. Good night."

Megan is still mulling over the dinner. She is dying to call Peter and debrief but figures that he won't clue her in on any negative feedback anyway. What is the use? Neither of them really cares. She realizes that she isn't overly concerned about Tiffany's opinion of her. She knows that Peter thinks she is the best thing since sliced bread.

She remembers Colin's loyalty issues. When she would vent to Colin about little disputes with his friends or family members, he would act like she was making a big deal out of nothing and barely listen to her. He just wanted the conflict to go away. Since Megan wanted everybody to like her, she would usually take Colin's advice and smooth over situations when she had done nothing wrong.

Things are different with Peter. For the first time in her life, she doesn't care if she is "liked" or not. With Peter by her side, she feels incredible strength and self-confidence. Even though they are a couple, she has never felt so secure as an individual. He brings out the best in her. It is invigorating, something she could never explain to anyone who hasn't experienced it before.

Meanwhile, back at his apartment, Peter opens a beer and starts to go through the stack of unopened mail on the counter. He sees a letter from the hospital in the city where he is to complete his fellowship year. His jaw drops when he reads that his space has been filled and they won't have room for him in the program in the fall. It is the only program in the city. Fortunately, he has applied to another hospital as backup. Unfortunately, this backup is back home—in Oklahoma. Peter is going to have to move.

TARA

Bret and Tara continue to date exclusively. There is never any frank discussion, but they are spending more and more time together. It has been more than two months and she usually sees him at least three nights a week. She is very happy.

One night, Bret asks her to accompany him to a friend's housewarming party. She has met most of the people there before, but there are also a few new couples. She chats easily with everyone and is starting to consider herself friends with several of his friends' girlfriends and spouses. She notices Bret is talking to a striking brunette. Tara asks one of her new friends who the woman is. "Oh, that's Corrine Keller. They used to work with each other. I think they may have dated, but don't worry, she's married."

"Whew, what a relief," Tara thinks. She makes her way over to Bret. When she stands next to him, it takes him a while to introduce her to the group he is talking too. "Oh, hey there," he says to Tara as he puts his arm around her. "This is my girlfriend, Tara. Tara, this is Deana and her husband Mark, and Corrine and her husband Ted." They all smile at her and make some brief, polite conversation before turning back to Bret and his latest project. Tara tries to join the conversation by mentioning she volunteers for the Historical Preservation Society—a group that is also very interested in the downtown revitalization project. "Actually, the HPS isn't involved with this one. We're working directly with the National Trust. Tara is an architecture buff but she doesn't work in the industry," Bret clarifies. Tara takes her cue and decides to spend her time with the group listening rather than speaking. After almost an hour, Tara excuses herself and makes her way back to their mutual friends across the room.

During the ride home, Tara tells Bret, "Boy, you seemed pretty engrossed in conversation with the same group of people all night. I think you said ten words to me." Bret apologizes but quickly says, "I have to talk a lot of business at these things. It's what keeps me in the loop. It's what wins me projects and that's important to me. You know how that goes."

Tara replies "I do, it's just that you were standing next to that Corrine woman for probably three hours. Did you two used to date?"

"Tara, she's married. I know her husband very well."

"She's also really gorgeous and seemed to be smiling a lot at you. I don't care if she's married, I've seen many married people act like they're not married."

"I can't control how other people act. And it seems like you're bent on thinking that something meaningless has meaning. It's just silly. We've been dating for a couple months. I haven't seen anybody else. Let's not forget, you were dating that guy who left the message on your machine up until a few weeks ago, right? We're with each other all of the time. If you can't trust me with a married former coworker, I don't know what to say." Tara decides to back off. "Listen, I'm just crabby because I'm tired," she explains.

Bret replies, "It's two in the morning. Let's just call it a night. We can get together tomorrow." The plan had been for her to stay over at his house. As Bret starts driving toward her house, Tara panics.

"Don't be mad at me," she says.

"I'm not mad," he replies, "I think we both just need some sleep." It's clear that he isn't going to change his mind. It's as if he wants to punish her in some way for her questions.

The next day, Tara's panic is replaced by anger. She is ticked off at Bret, and she thinks about *The List*. She thought that Bret was loyal. Since they started dating, he is always ready to listen to her work woes and take her side. But last night, she noticed some disloyal behavior. He left her on her own for most of the evening and spent a good amount of time with a former flame. He also went out of his way to point out to his friends that, basically, she didn't know what she was talking about. Sure, when he finally got around to introducing her, he said she was his "girlfriend" but it seemed like he would have been just as happy being at the party without her.

Later that week, while Bret's out running errands, Tara decides to use his computer to order a birthday gift for her mom. She turns on the monitor and Bret's e-mail inbox is displayed. She sees an e-mail from Corrine Keller. The preview is open and it reads, "Bret, it was great to see you. Maybe we can get together for lunch the next time you're on my side of town. Best, Corrine."

Tara says out loud to the computer, "What the hell is this?" Bret knows that she uses his computer, so he can't accuse her of snooping or sneaking around. Just then Bret comes back, "Hey what's up?"

Tara tries to remain calm. "Um, I was just ordering my mom's birthday gift online and your inbox popped up. Look who e-mailed you." Bret leans over her shoulder to read the note.

"Hmm," he says. "I wouldn't worry about that. I don't know what her deal is. There's only one girl I want to have lunch with and she's sitting right here, so what do you say? You want to head out and grab something and maybe do some shopping?"

Tara isn't ready to let it go. "Bret, this really bothers me. What's her deal?"

"There is no deal. I'm not going to e-mail her back, so let's just drop it."

Tara is silent.

"Listen, to prove it, I will e-mail her back and tell her I'm not interested. Here, I'll do it right now." And he did. It read, "Corrine, thanks for the message. I don't think my girlfriend would be happy if I had lunch with you! Say hi to Ted—Bret."

What could Tara say? He nipped it right in the bud. Still, she couldn't help but think that if he wouldn't have spent so much time with Corrine at the party, it wouldn't have been an issue. She decided to brush off the nagging feeling she had. Bret had demonstrated his loyalty in his own way.

A few days after the e-mail situation, Tara runs into her friend Kim at the grocery store. They chat for a bit and Tara awkwardly asks how Patrick is doing. "Great!" Kim replies. She holds out her left hand: "We're getting married!"

CHRISTINE

Barry and Christine know that it is time to prepare their family and friends for their big announcement. They decide that it would be too shocking to blurt out, "We're getting married!" right away. They reason that people are always much more supportive when they feel they are a part of the process.

Barry meets Christine's parents, and they love him. After years of watching their daughter succeed in business, they enjoy watching her succeed in love. They have met Christine's boyfriends here and there over time, but Barry seems different. He isn't the one they pictured Christine with in some ways, but in other ways he is the perfect complement to their daughter. Christine's mother pulls her aside and tells her, "You've never looked so happy."

"Well, I've never been happier. And I think it may be time to pull your wedding gown out of the closet and see if I can squeeze into it." Much to Christine's surprise, her mother isn't shocked at all. After all, when she met her husband forty-two years earlier, they were engaged within two months and married two months after that.

A couple of weeks later, Christine meets Barry's parents at their lake house. His family is a lot of fun, and his mother and stepfather seem very normal. Barry has a married older brother and a younger single brother. His brother's wife is a paralegal and she enjoys talking shop with Christine. They all convince Christine that they can teach her to water-ski in an afternoon and take great pride when they accomplish their goal.

She notices that everybody in Barry's family understands the art of conversation. They all ask her a lot of questions and bring up topics that everybody is interested in. She happily realizes that Barry is close to his family and that weekends at the lake will be a part of their married life. Barry's sister-in-law takes her aside and tells her, "I hope we aren't scaring you off. When I first came up here, I got nervous about having to be with everybody all the time. But it's not like that. They are always happy to see us, but they never guilt or pressure us." Christine is touched by this gesture. She feels that she is wanted and that she belongs here. When the women of the family corner Barry alone, they rave about Christine. He tells them, "Well, I think we could use a lawyer in the family. I just wish we had a jeweler!" Barry's mother is quick to point out that she has saved her wedding ring from Barry's late father and that, "It's ready when you are." Barry is touched and relieved. He knows that Christine will truly appreciate the sentiment.

When they get back to town, Barry tells Christine that his family loves her. The lack of tension on both sides of the family is a relief, and is really just icing on the cake. When their friends learn of their relationship, some may think they are moving too fast, but they are ready to get officially engaged. Christine has to go out of town for a short business trip so Barry decides to call a few friends that he hasn't seen in a while. They meet up at the local bar to have some beer, play darts, and watch a hockey game. Barry learns that one of the other guys has also has found a serious girlfriend and another is finally getting married to his girlfriend of four years. Barry says, "Yeah, I've been seeing someone too. I think we may be getting married soon."

Everyone is really surprised. It's only been a few short months since they've last seen Barry, and he didn't have a girlfriend at the time. Some of the guys are congratulatory in a joking sort of way, "Hey Barry! That's great, you found your sugar mama."

Another friend pipes in, "Dude, what's the hurry? You barely know each other." Barry knows this friend broke up with his long-time girlfriend about nine months ago, and tries to brush it off. Later, as they are walking out of the bar, his friend approaches him again. "Barry, I'm just trying to look out for you, man. I'm just saying that you don't need to rush into things. I don't want to see you go through another divorce."

Barry replies, "I get that, but you don't know Christine. Besides I'm older and wiser now. I know what I'm doing."

Barry's buddy is bugged. He just can't believe that Barry would get engaged to a woman he's only known for a couple of months. It seems like all of his friends are dropping like flies. He's finally a free man and now this. He gets in his car and picks up his cell phone. He stares at it and thinks for a second. Then he dials his ex-girlfriend's number, "Hey, it's me. I just wanted to see how you're doing. I've been thinking about you and wondering how things are going. Give me a call, Megan." Colin snaps his phone shut and lets out a sigh. He feels better already.

WRAP-UP

Loyalty is the key to a happy marriage. Sure, there are times to play devil's advocate, and sometimes there will be slip-ups, but you know that he is your rock. And you are his. If you find yourself feeling insecure because of something you said or did during the early part of the relationship, you cannot check off this box. With a List Man, there are no worries. You feel carefree and peaceful about your relationship. If the man you are seeing criticizes you, lies to you, cheats on you, or doesn't stick up for you—you need to dump him. Even if he does all the other things on *The List*, this is a deal breaker.

Remember that a List Man:

☑ Should be your biggest fan, not your harshest critic.

☑ Should take your side on matters great and small, especially during the early weeks of dating.

☑ Will never let other people come between you.

NINE

List

Item 7:

HE TALKS ABOUT MARRYING
YOU IN CONCRETE TERMS
AND PROPOSES—OR LETS
YOU KNOW HIS INTENTIONS

By the time you've reached this point, something magical has happened: the Fairy Tale. You go to bed at night secure in his love for you and wake up in the morning feeling the exact same way. Somehow, without even realizing how it happened, you both know that you are getting married to each other.

Marriage is a natural topic that should come up a lot if you are dating a List Man. When a man is courting you, the subject of marriage will come up naturally within thirty days and sometimes in less time than that. The actions he takes will all be to one end: to spend as much time as he can with you, so nobody else can have you, and so he can convince you that he is deserving of your heart and hand forever. When you sound a man's Alarm, all he thinks about is how you fit into his future, and marriage is on his mind.

Some women are convinced that discussing marriage is a monumental ordeal, but that's not necessarily true. Remember, Prince Charming saw Cinderella, stalked her, and they lived happily ever after. We never saw him actually propose. It just happened.

You may think that early proposals only happen to other people, and so you say things like, "Well, that is crazy. Nobody gets engaged that fast." But for every couple you know who has dated, shacked up, and hung out for five years before heading down the aisle, you know a happily married couple who met and made a commitment to get married within thirty days.

The Language of a List Man

If you always remember that men are action-based creatures rather than verbal beings, it will not be hard to decode what they're saying when it comes to commitment. A List Man will *not* say anything like this to you:

> ▷ "Yeah, I definitely want to get married someday."
> ▷ "I really admire my parent's marriage, and that's what I want to find."
> ▷ "I can't wait to get married and have kids."
> ▷ "I love kids and want what my sister/brother/best friend has."

These statements are vague and, once again, they are about *him* and not *you*.

When The Alarm sounds, a List Man balances the present with the future. He is enjoying every moment with you and, at the same time, seeing you as part of his future. If you live across town from each other, he will start thinking about how you will remedy that when you are married. If he knows that he may be transferred for work, he knows that his plans will include you. If he had hoped to take an expensive vacation to Japan in a year, he realizes that it may not happen.

Mary's best friend from college, Dave, had to rethink his future quickly. An attorney, he had just quit a big job on the East Coast to try his luck in Seattle. He called Mary to say that he would be passing through Minneapolis on the way to his new adventure. Two days later, Mary met Linda, a fabulous woman, whom she thought would be a perfect match for Dave. She told Linda, "Come to my house this Saturday, and I will introduce you to your husband." When Dave took his first look at Linda, he quipped, "I hear we're getting married, any history of mental illness?" The next day, he took her on a romantic picnic. Then he left for Seattle. After a couple of weeks of daily phone conversations with Dave, Linda decided to accept his invitation to attend his mother's wedding. She flew to Seattle, and it was there that he made his intentions clear. Dave moved to Minneapolis and they were "officially" engaged four months later. (PS: They have been married for six years and have a son named Jack.)

There are hundreds of different scenarios that a List Man will mull over now that he has met "the one." If a List Man has a more brazen personality and is sure that he has won you over, he will think out loud with you about what is on his mind. As Jon told Mary within two days, "I just want you to know that my intention is to win your heart."

If a List Man is more cautious and is still trying to make sure you are on the same page, he will "slip" and give you clues that he wants to marry you. Once he realizes that you feel the same way, he will be relieved and your dialogue about the future will become very open and natural. Todd "slipped" and told Sheila: "It's your choice, but I would like it if you stayed home with our kids."

There's a subtlety, but the message is clear. He didn't say, "I would like it if *my wife* stayed home with kids"; he was specific. A List Man will make it clear that it is *you* whom he pictures by his side.

Sometimes the woman beats the List Man to the punch. She blurts out something about getting married.

Sue, happily married for ten years, explains:

"I had bought Shane a Christmas present (a ring). I am a terrible secret keeper, so I showed it to him early. He didn't really like it, so I joked that we should exchange it for a wedding ring. He agreed. That was all it took."

While it is best to let the List Man bring up marriage, if you slip up, it won't scare him off. Why would it? You sounded his Alarm weeks ago, and it is the only thing on his mind. Since he knows that you are the one, he won't be put off if you bring up marriage. He may even be relieved.

The Thirty-Day Guarantee

The only thing we know for sure is that if you have sounded a man's Alarm, you will know where you stand within thirty days. After thirty days, he knows everything about you there is to know. He knows that another six weeks or six months isn't going to change a thing. Whether he thinks out loud, slips, or hears you blurt out something about marriage and engages in a conversation, a List Man will feel comfortable talking about marriage because you have sounded The Alarm. He won't hold his cards too close to the vest because he knows that time is of the essence. Once he knows that you want to marry him too, he will breathe a sigh of relief because he has accomplished the biggest mission in his life.

Remember David and Ashley? They discussed marriage quickly. Ashley says:

> "Neither one of us officially brought it up. It just naturally began to flow into our conversations by our saying things like, 'If we're supposed to be together,' and eventually, 'I want to be with you forever.' I never had to drop a hint or issue an ultimatum; we were using each date— not each month or year—as a litmus test for whether or not this was the real thing."

Once they knew that they wanted to get married, David and Ashley checked into booking an event facility. But nothing was available soon enough.

> *"Finally, we made the decision that we weren't waiting any longer. We were going to elope. We booked some plane tickets at five o'clock one afternoon, and were jetting off by nine-thirty that same night. We were married exactly three months from our first date."*

Now *that's* romantic!

Early marriage proposals are romantic because they lack pretense and planning. Many couples that use *The List* may not have the most over-the-top proposals in the world. He may not take you on a hot-air balloon ride or propose at the Super Bowl with your face broadcast to 50 million people. When a man hasn't dragged his feet, he doesn't have anything to make up for!

Often, there was never even a real proposal for *List* couples. Jeff, happily married for ten years, relates that on their third date, his now wife said, "I wish I could find a man who would let me keep my last name." His reply was, "I think I can deal with that." And that was it. From that day on, they both knew that they would get married. And a year later, they did.

Larry, introduced in Chapter 3, reports:

> *"I never really proposed marriage to Gail. And I can't even remember the moment it was finalized. I just remember that we took a trip to New York, and during our flight we looked at each other and said, 'Let's make a list of people we will invite to the wedding.' We just both*

*knew we were going to get married. The wedding was three months
later. When a guy is ready to get married, he doesn't waste time with
the logistics."*

Most of these couples simply discuss that they are getting
engaged, talk about a potential wedding date, and move forward. It
can be as simple as driving to the jewelry store after work and buying
a ring.

Dawn remembers:

*"It wasn't a big moment for us. He says he knew he wanted to marry
me when I casually mentioned during an early date that I could see
myself spending the future with him. I am not sure what the exact
words were, but, as I recall, the statement was not about marriage
directly. A few weeks later when I asked him to look at an apartment
with me (I was planning to move in alone, of course), we went to
a cafe afterward to discuss the apartment, and he told me that
he didn't think I needed to sign a year's lease. That's when I knew he
wanted to marry me. We were officially engaged two months later."*

If your man wants to put together an elaborate proposal, that's
great. But it certainly isn't necessary (and it can be a little nauseating
for everybody but you). He is excited to start his married life with
you and doesn't need to make a Hollywood production out of it. On
the way home from a trip after a few months of dating, Caroline and
Justin (remember them from List Items 1 and 3?) started talking about
marriage. According to Caroline,

"There was no big revelation about getting married. It seemed a natural progression to merge our lives into something cohesive and permanent. I remember talking about whether we wanted to have children."

At this point, Justin made his intentions clear. Five months later, they were engaged.

Sid remembers discussing marriage early in their relationship:

"I actually was talking to Tricia on the phone about four weeks into the relationship when I brought it up. I basically said that I was not interested in dating her for the sake of dating but was pursuing her toward marriage. I think there was a moment of stunned silence. I wasn't sure if she had dropped the phone. She mentioned she had commitment issues and I just said, 'That's fine, I'm willing to fight for you.' I don't know where that came from, it just came out."

If you still don't believe that men will talk about marriage in concrete terms within the first thirty days of courtship, here's another example. About three weeks after Deborah and Norm (from List Items 1 and 6) went on their first date, she received flowers at work from another guy she had been casually dating.

"I think that sent Norm over the edge. Norm sent flowers to the office, and called up Tiffany's and had them two-day ship an engagement ring, sight unseen. When the ring came, he walked to my office and put the blue box on my desk. He asked me to marry him. Norm figured that the only way to stop me from dating other people

*was to ask me to marry him. I said yes, and had to cancel a date
to the opera with another guy. I'm the only girl I know who had to
call someone and say, 'I'm sorry I have to cancel our date, but I'm
engaged.'"*

Why the Thirty-Day Rule?

When a man doesn't bring up marriage within thirty days, it is
tempting to start questioning *The List*. After all, he has already
checked off six items! Make sure you review all of the previous *List*
items carefully. Maybe he really didn't spend all of his free time with
you and you were willing to make excuses for this. Maybe he got
too comfortable and brought you into his social circle rather than
woo you one-on-one. Or, maybe he doesn't love you for who you
are and isn't loyal to you. If you haven't been true to *The List* and
have been making excuses for sub-par behavior up to this point,
you need to reevaluate and restart your search for a List Man. In
your quest to make excuses, you will look for loopholes. You will
inevitably know some married couples who are happy despite the
fact that the man didn't do one item on *The List*, let alone all seven.
If you ask these people whether they believe that all of this can
happen within thirty days, they may say things like: "Well, we dated
for five years and got married."

People can still get married without using *The List*. You aren't in
their shoes, and it is not for you to judge their marriage.

It is likely that the woman in those relationships was perfectly
content dating for a few years before a commitment was made. It
doesn't mean that one way is right and another way is wrong. *The List*

isn't about other people's philosophies on courtship and marriage; it is about what will work for *you*. If you don't want to waste time and take the risk that you haven't sounded The Alarm, *The List* will work for you.

It is more important to stay focused on your own goals throughout all the items on *The List*. List Item 7 is a crucial point for you, and you don't need the distraction or the counterpoint from anyone who doesn't understand *The List*. If you need support when you are using *The List,* seek the ongoing counsel of a friend or family member who met and married a List Man. She will immediately "get" *The List* and will be thrilled that somebody has defined her own Fairy Tale courtship. Call this person any time that you feel doubtful about *The List*. She will help you determine if you are on the right path.

From your end, thirty days is a major milestone in a relationship. The only thing that will come from letting another thirty days—or another six months—go by is wasted time. Avoid the attachment issues and timeline tampering that can come with hanging onto a non-List Man. If you didn't have *The List*, this would be the point where you would start saying things such as:

- ▷ "We need to take this to the next level."
- ▷ "Do you see a future with me?"
- ▷ "Where do you see this going?"
- ▷ "I'm not interested in dating, I'm interested in marriage."
- ▷ "You're ____ old, isn't it time to get engaged?"
- ▷ "I need to know where I stand."

Or, you would think "it is too soon" and you would wait until enough time has passed to issue an ultimatum. But with *The List*, you know that when a man meets the woman of his dreams, there is no need to do a pulse-check or prod him to find out how he feels about you. If you have reached this point and the subject of marriage has not come up easily, you need to walk away with grace and dignity. This is never an easy thing but since you have only invested thirty days in the relationship, you can do it. You simply need to tell him the truth:

"I just don't think this is what I want or need."

Or

"I can't explain why, but this isn't right for me."

He may be completely baffled. After all, he doesn't know about The Alarm and he doesn't know about *The List*. But you don't owe him any explanation—and you certainly don't have time for it. You are in control and you know what you are doing.

If you have gotten this far on *The List*, and you haven't been making excuses, you won't have anything to worry about. If you are with a List Man, you won't even have to stop and assess this item, it will all happen naturally. It is key that you know his intentions or be engaged to him within thirty days because you can start your life together on a high note. When you first meet the List Man, you are filled with so much hope and excitement that you just may burst. Well, it turns out that a List Man feels the same way when he meets you. You set off The Alarm and, for the first time in his life, he isn't analyzing or shutting down his emotions. He isn't thinking, "It's too soon," or "What's the hurry." He is thinking:

- ▷ "I love her."
- ▷ "I'm ready."
- ▷ "This is it."

The List Man also knows that as time goes on, the intensity curve will even out. The initial thrill of meeting and falling in love will compete with other daily pressures that will cause a loss of momentum. Besides, if he waits, somebody else will steal you away. It's time to close the deal.

If he proposes when you are on a "high" as a couple, he is giving your marriage the best possible launching pad. It starts at the highest possible point and levels off at the highest possible point. Most of the happily married people you meet started with an early marriage proposal. If you doubt this, start asking around.

A List Man can't imagine spending the rest of his life without you. Being with you has been a dream for him and he wants it to continue. He wants more—much more. He wants to close the deal so he can relax. If he knows that you really want to get engaged ASAP, he will propose. If he knows that you want to elope to Las Vegas in a week, he will do it. If he knows that you want to wait a few more months— or a year—before getting engaged, he will make sure you know that he intends to ask for your hand whenever you are ready. The bottom line is that he will do what *you* want to do. It has always been, and still is, about making you happy.

LIFE IN LISTOPIA

MEGAN

After a late-night run to the ice cream shop, Megan returns home and listens to a message on her answering machine. It's Colin! She stands still in silent shock for a good two minutes. She plays the message back three times: "Hey, it's me. I just wanted to see how you're doing. I've been thinking about you and wondering how things are going. Give me a call, Megan."

It has been nine months since they broke up, and she hasn't even seen him, let alone talked to him, in months. She remembers the early months after they broke up and how difficult it was to erase him from her life. She cringes when she thinks about the two times she broke down and called him. The first time, she left a message on his answering machine (a very similar message to the one he just left on hers). The second time, he picked up the phone and they had an awkward conversation. She also remembers how she was still thinking about Colin right up until the time she met Peter. She is tempted to call him back to feed her ego, but she doesn't. It isn't worth it, and it isn't healthy. No, her best revenge for the years she wasted on her relationship with Colin is to not give him the time of day. The old Megan would have thought, "Wow, he must really still love me," or, "Well, we must be 'meant to be.'" She sees through the whole charade. Colin doesn't miss her—he is just lonely. "Selfish, selfish, selfish," she thinks. She smiles and picks up the phone to call Peter.

Peter is in the shower and doesn't hear the phone. It's late and his mind is racing. He is thinking about his imminent move to Oklahoma.

He doesn't want to shift from a wonderful, romantic time with Megan to making huge, realistic decisions. He knows that she loves the city and has lived in this part of the country her entire life. She would probably never want to go to Oklahoma. He can't remember how marriage came up or when, exactly, but he knows that they are both on the same page. He decides that he needs to talk to Megan about Oklahoma as soon as possible. Tomorrow will be spent with his sister, who never seems interested in finding her way around the city herself.

The next day, Megan is glad to have the excuse of attending a bridal shower. She really doesn't want to spend more time with Tiffany and company than she has to, but when Peter calls that afternoon, she agrees to meet them out for dinner again.

When Megan gets to the restaurant, she notices a change in Tiffany. Tiffany is asking her all kinds of questions about herself. At the end of most of the questions, Tiffany smiles and says, "How nice." A good friend of Megan's is from the South, and she warned Megan that "How nice" is usually code for either "I could care less" or "We have absolutely nothing in common." Megan continues to be polite and gets through the dinner. She bids them all farewell for the evening and looks forward to tomorrow, when she'll have Peter back to herself.

To her surprise, Peter calls a few hours later and asks if he can come over. "What about your family?" she asks him.

"I've got that covered," is his only reply.

When he arrives, Megan asks, "Well, what was the verdict?"

Peter assures her that his sister thought that she was "very nice."

"Oh, how nice." Megan replies sarcastically. They laugh together.

Peter hesitates. "Meg, we need to talk."

Uh, oh, Megan thinks, *the worst statement ever to come from a man's lips.* "What?"

"I have to move at the end of June. I have to go back to Oklahoma for a year for my fellowship training."

Megan is stunned. Here she has just met his somewhat-difficult sister and now he is moving back there? "How long have you known this?" Megan demands.

"I found out last night when I went through my mail. I'm completely surprised. I just assumed I'd be accepted into the program here."

"So you'll be there for a year. You're not moving there for good, right?" she asks.

"I don't know. But Oklahoma is a great place for my specialty. It's not that I like it there or that it would be my number-one choice of where to live, but it has a great hospital where I have connections. I applied there as a backup before I met you."

"I've done long-distance relationships, and they don't work. I want to see you every day, not once a month," she says.

He hugs her and says, "That's how I feel. I love you and I know that I want to be with you forever. I want you to move with me. If you absolutely hate it, we can figure something else out."

"I can't just pick up and move halfway across the country. We're not even engaged," Megan says.

"Megan, listen to me. Did you hear what I just said? I said I love you and want to be with you forever. I want to marry you. Will you marry me?"

Megan is stunned. Peter is a true List Man. She knew that they would be together, but it's happening so fast. Peter hasn't even met her family—there hasn't been a good occasion to introduce him to them. She would be leaving her job and family and moving to a different state. Everything is a blur, but this doesn't prevent her from accepting a proposal from her List Man. She knows that she will be happy as long as she is with Peter.

"Yes!" she almost shouts. She can't believe it; she will be married right after her twenty-seventh birthday.

TARA

After Tara sees her friend Kim at the store, she is in utter disbelief. She only gave her Patrick's number a couple of months ago. "Obviously, he must have been really desperate and would have married the first girl that would have him," she thinks. Still, she feels really strange. She had set a goal to get married by the time she is thirty-two. She is already thirty-one now, and here she could have been married in a few months had she stuck with Patrick. She reasoned that she had followed her heart with Bret and because she did, fate intervened and brought together two people who belonged together. She wished the best for Kim and Patrick, really she did. Patrick was definitely a List Man, just not her List Man.

Things are still percolating with Bret. She still sees him three nights a week. He has a very hectic work schedule and sees her whenever he can. Usually she has dinner with him once during the middle of the week and they almost always spend Friday and Saturday night together. At the beginning of the relationship, she felt this was a List relationship for sure. But she is looking for some forward momentum. She had hoped that by now they would be together 24/7, but that hasn't happened. Bret lets her hang at his pad on the weekend afternoons when he is busy, but she usually ends up going back to her place or killing time by shopping or doing other errands. Bret isn't great about calling and keeping her posted on day-to-day stuff. Once he gets to his office, he is totally engrossed in his work and forgets to call. She has never dated a creative type like Bret and knows that he just isn't ever going to be the type of guy who calls her to talk about nothing.

She is always happy when she's with Bret. She loves to hear about his week, and he's a great listener and gives her emotional support for her work stories. When she's not with him, she's thinking about him and what he's doing. She sometimes calls him at work or on his cell phone just to check in, and he is usually very sweet unless he's in the middle of something at the office. She has no worries that he's unfaithful to her, but she is frustrated that they can't be with each other more often. She tries to talk to Bret about her need to spend more time with him, but he either changes the subject or tells her that he loves her and that things will get better when he is done with the downtown project. It is so wonderful to hear him say he loves her. Still, she feels very uneasy when they are apart.

Tara puts her insecurities aside because she and Bret are approaching a major milestone: She is going to meet his family. He has invited her to a cousin's wedding on the East Coast. She knows that a good review from his parents and siblings will certainly help her cause, as Bret is very close with all of them. She finishes work on Friday and meets him at the airport.

After they arrive at the hotel, they change and immediately head down to the lobby bar where friends and family of the bride and groom are gathering. Bret warmly embraces old buddies and relatives and is having a fantastic time. Tara stands back waiting for her introduction. Bret always introduces her as "my girlfriend, Tara." Everyone smiles, shakes her hand, and seems genuinely interested in meeting her. After a glass of wine, she easily joins the conversation and seems to be winning some new friends with her charm. She sees Bret make his way to the door to two pretty blondes holding toddlers. Tara waits for Bret to wave her over, but he doesn't, so she decides to make her way over to the reunion. "Hey, Tara, this is my sister Tracy and my other sister Amanda. These are my nephews and my newest niece," Bret proudly exclaims to Tara. The kids throw themselves at Bret and he hugs them and puts one on his shoulders while the other is crawling through his legs. The sisters are laughing and both smile at Tara. "They just love their Uncle Bret. Tara, it is so nice to meet you. We've heard a lot about you."

"So where are your good-for-nothing husbands?" Bret teases.

"Our wonderful husbands are watching the end of the game upstairs, they'll be down in a minute," Tracy replies. Tara is instantly comforted that his family "has heard a lot about her." She oohs and ahhs over the baby girl and offers to help them with all of their baby gear. They find a spot to sit in the busy lounge and soon two more couples walk over. It's his two older brothers and their wives sans children, who are up in one of the rooms with a nanny, Tara is informed. They all smile and shake Tara's hand and are soon laughing and telling her stories about Bret from childhood, high school, and college. "He was the baby, you see, and totally spoiled by our parents. He got away with murder; we all wanted to kill him," they all chime in.

Tara is having a great time. The rest of the night is a blur. She meets a ton of people, with the exception of Bret's parents, who are at the rehearsal dinner. After a few hours of hanging out, Tara announces that she's going to turn in early so she has enough energy to keep up with them tomorrow. Bret stays downstairs with everyone and gets back to the room around 1:00 A.M. Tara wakes up and asks if he had a good time. "Oh, this is the best. I forgot how much fun I can have with the fam. I think I heard a hundred times how funny and smart and cute you are." They kiss and have a nice little tryst in the posh hotel room.

The next day is the wedding. It is beautiful—probably the classiest wedding that Tara has attended. She tears up as she always does and notices that Bret squeezes her hand a little harder when the bride and groom take their vows. At the reception, she finally meets Bret's parents. Just like his siblings, they are very gracious and kind to Tara. His mother even asks a few leading questions, "So Bret, these weddings sure are fun. I hope we won't have to wait too long to have a party of our own!" They all laugh, and Tara is delighted that they feel so at ease talking about these kinds of things in front of her. Bret tells her several times during the evening that at his wedding he will "be a bit more minimal in the decorations" or that he will "wear a suit instead of a tux" or that "he will have both a jazz band *and* disco band." It seems as if Bret has given a lot of thought to his wedding, and Tara can only hope that has something to do with her. Toward the end of the night, when they are slow dancing, Tara asks Bret, "So can you see this for us someday?" Bret smiles and kisses her. She feels so warm and happy.

The next morning, they say their goodbyes to Bret's family. When they get back to the city late Sunday night, Bret quickly tells the driver "We're going to make two stops," and gives him both of the addresses.

Tara asks him, "Oh, do you need to get some clothes for work tomorrow and meet me at my place later?"

Bret replies, "It's been a long weekend and I'm just really exhausted."

"Oh, okay." Tara replies. She is shocked and upset. They just spent a wonderful, perfect weekend together. She met his family, who loved her; he told her at least ten times how much he loved her, and he even talked about marriage for Pete's sake! But now he doesn't even want to go home with her because he needs his Sunday night wind-down? She sits in silence, burning up inside. When the taxi pulls up in her driveway she says, "You know what? This is bull. I can't believe this is the end to the weekend. Stay in your precious house by your precious self and why don't you give me a call the next time you feel like being around me." She slams the door and walks away.

She hates feeling this way—so needy, so desperate, so out of control. *The List* says he should have proposed—or at least have told her when he planned on proposing—by now. They talked about marriage at the wedding, but she knows in her heart it wasn't in any concrete terms. She loves Bret, and he says he loves her. She can't go back to being alone again. What is she going to do? She checks her mail and sees an invitation to Patrick and Kim's upcoming nuptials—great. There's another invitation, it's from one of her clients—an attorney named Christine whom she's known for years. Christine is getting married? She didn't even know Christine had a boyfriend. Tara hangs her head and sobs. Where the hell was that *List* book anyway? It's time for a dustoff.

CHRISTINE

When Christine gets back from her business trip, Barry picks her up at the airport. Christine notices something on the passenger's seat when she gets in the car. It's an old white ring box tied with a pretty blue ribbon. Christine has known for weeks that this was coming, but she thought they agreed to shop together for the ring when she got back in town. She is pleasantly surprised to find a beautiful antique diamond ring in the box. Barry explains that it is his mother's from his late father, and that his family loved her so much that they wanted her to have it and so did he. She cries, surprising even herself, since this is far from a shocking moment. But the sentimentality of the ring and Barry's adorable grin makes Christine so happy she can't hold back the tears. She can't believe this is happening to her. She remembers the first night that she met Barry at the bookstore. She remembers how she introduced herself and left an opening for Barry to approach her. She is so happy that she got outside of her little box and took a risk.

That night, they decide they will get married at Barry's parents' lake house in eight weeks. She laughs, thinking about what her coworkers would think. They'll probably speculate that she's pregnant.

Christine has always thought she would have a very posh, sophisticated wedding at an expensive boutique hotel or maybe at a country club by the water. But now that she has found Barry, she just doesn't care all that much about the trappings. She is not interested in spending all of her savings trying to impress people; it just doesn't fit the "new Christine."

In the midst of the planning, Christine makes plans to have

lunch with Tara, who worked for the marketing firm Christine's firm employed. She and Tara have become friends over the years.

The minute she sits down at the restaurant, Tara immediately gushes, "Gosh, I haven't seen you forever. You look great, and I can't believe you're getting married! I mean the last time we talked about men, you had just had that terrible date with that guy at the boat show. Tell me everything!"

Christine explains their crazy, quick courtship, the miraculous speed of the engagement, and how it was "So easy. It just happened." Tara tells her that she is thrilled and can't wait for the wedding. She inquires about her bridal registry and they talk more about the wedding plans.

"So am I going to meet that architect at the wedding? The last we talked, you had just gone out on a spectacular first date. You sounded head over heels. Are you still seeing him?"

Tara nods, "Yeah, his name's Bret. It's progressing I guess. We're exclusive with each other, but I'm just worried it's not going anywhere. I'm very scared about wasting time on him. But I'm very much wrapped up in the relationship, if you know what I mean. I've met his parents, and he gushes over me when we are together. One day I am convinced that he wants to marry me, then the next I just don't know."

Christine listens patiently and then says, "You know Tara, I'm almost forty, and you're still a babe of thirty or so. So listen to an old wise woman. Have you ever heard of *The List*?"

Tara's jaw drops, "You did *The List*? So did I! But you're getting married and I don't know where I'm going. It's funny because I pulled out the book the other day and I think I may have inadvertently let

Bret slip through without really performing some of the actions."

"Well let's go through them," Christine says, ordering a bottle of wine for the task. "It's Friday, and we're going to make this lunch last until happy hour. We certainly work enough overtime to do that once in a while." Both ladies call in to their offices and make excuses. Then, the dishing begins.

"So, what are your "'must haves'?'"

"Well, I didn't really do that. I know that I want the right things. And it's not like I'm picky." Christine arches her eyebrow and gives Tara a knowing look. They both laugh.

"Okay, moving right along ... did he make the first move?" Christine continues.

"We were set up on a blind date, so that one was hard to qualify."

"Okay. How about List Item 2? How long did it take for him to call you?"

"It took a while, now that you mention it. He had my phone number for weeks before he ever contacted me, but he was away in China on business—it seemed like a valid excuse. He didn't ask me out on that first call, but we had a good conversation. He actually canceled our first date once we had one planned. Wow, I sound stupid already."

"Well, he certainly wasn't too concerned with impressing you. Did he make the first date easy and fun?"

"Well, he asked me out on my answering machine leaving me to guess whether or not the date was a 'go.' That was definitely not fun. But, our first date was a dream date, probably the best date I've ever been on. The one I talked to you about the next day at lunch, remember? Black-tie, martinis beforehand at the Meridian Club, he introduced me to all of his friends, was extremely polite. Made sure

I was included and complimented me throughout the evening. I felt like I was flying on air after that date."

"But was it a He-date?" Christine asks.

Tara starts to laugh, "Watching him get an award for some architect-of-the-year honor? Yeah, that's probably the ultimate He-date, huh?"

They both started laughing.

"And deep inside, I knew that was the case. But it is so hard to change your thinking," Tara explains.

"So after that first date, did he contact you within twenty-four hours to set up the next date?" Christine continues.

"Yes! He did actually call me the next day and set up a date for that same evening. I know I'm not totally crazy. He did do some things right!" replies Tara.

"So what did you do for that date?" Christine asks.

"We had sushi, hung out with some of his friends, and I went home with him that night. Nice touch, don't you think?" Tara says self-effacingly.

"So he was out with his friends on those early dates? That's definitely not one-on-one," Christine points out.

"Well, they happened to be at the restaurant, and he invited them over, but yeah, you're right. They hung out with us the rest of the night. Come to think of it, I've spent more time with some of his friends than I have with him," Tara says.

"Did he want to spend all of his time with you, and does he still?" Christine asks.

"Um, no, I would definitely say no to that one," Tara replies.

Christine goes on, without interjecting any judgment, "Okay, how about demonstrating unconditional loyalty?"

"That was a really hard one to judge. But, there was an incident at a party where he kind of brushed me off in front of his friends. Not to mention the fact that he spent hours talking to a married ex-girlfriend," Tara says.

"Okay. Next. You've been dating for a few months. Has he talked about marrying you in any concrete terms, or has he told you his intentions?" Christine is a regular Katie Couric now, firing away *The List* criteria.

"Well, at the wedding, he talked a lot about how *his* wedding will be. And I asked him if he could see us getting married. But, come to think of it, he really didn't answer me. Unless great sex later that night was an answer!"

By now, the wine is hitting and they both start laughing again.

"Boy, I'm listening to myself and thinking 'what a fool'! I could have cut my losses weeks ago." Tara is shaking her head.

Christine looks her straight in the eye. "Isn't it funny what happens when you peel the onion a bit? It doesn't matter that he's great looking, has a great job, or lives in a great house, does it? He's not great at all. He's not 'the one,' and by dating him, you're keeping yourself away from your true love. I'm envious that you can see the light at a young age; I didn't get it until I was thirty-nine. Try to find dating prospects at my age. It becomes a real challenge. I got so lucky with Barry. He's six years younger than I am, divorced, has a steady but sort of a boring job, but he's my soul mate. He did everything on *The List,* and all I had to do was stay out of the way and let it happen. You will meet your prince, I promise. But you know what you need to do first so that he can find you."

Tara is able to see clearly now that she needs to break up with Bret. And for some reason, she *wants* to break up with him so she can get on with her life. She realizes that it will be hard to let go of the fantasy, but she doesn't want to be sitting here a year from now having the same conversation.

"Thank you for your wisdom, Yoda! Really, this has been great. I'm so happy for you, and I can't wait for the wedding. Oh and by the way, I'll be sending in my RSVP soon, for one, no guest."

"Good girl. By the way, I'll be introducing you to Barry's brother Alan at the wedding. He's thirty-one, adorable, very single, and I know he wants to get married!"

WRAP-UP

If he's done everything on *The List*, you don't have anything to fret about. He will state his intentions or propose within thirty days. And he will do whatever makes you happy. Ultimatums are never necessary with List Men. If you sounded The Alarm, he will meet the last requirement of *The List*.

If a man doesn't state his intentions or propose within thirty days, it is likely that he really didn't do all the things on *The List*. Don't doubt yourself or *The List*. Don't waste time explaining *The List* or issuing an ultimatum. You haven't sounded The Alarm, and there is nothing you can do to change that. Be thankful that you have only invested thirty days in the relationship. Ask your Fairy Tale friends to support you because you will have to move on.

Remember:

☑ It is so easy for months to turn into years.

☑ If you are with the wrong man, your chances of meeting the right man are slim to none.

☑ You don't have time to waste.

BONUS! LIFE IN LISTOPIA

Christine and Barry's wedding day promises to be perfect. The sky is blue, and the temperature is expected to reach the upper seventies.

When Tara arrives, she smiles to herself. It seems that Christine's "low-key" wedding has managed to get a bit out of control. It is downright elegant. Tara isn't surprised by this, however. She never pictured her urban friend barefoot by the shores of Moose Lake. A long, white runner divides the rows of white chairs. The "altar" is a gazebo overlooking the lake. A big white tent is set up in the side yard. The inside is completely decked out with fabric, flowers, and twinkling lights. The apricot and purple flowers and accents are perfect for the fall day.

After her lunch-turned-happy-hour with Christine of a few weeks before, Tara knew that she needed to really think about her relationship with Bret. She wanted to give him another chance. She decided to call him and talk things over. With the wine clouding her judgment, she called him from the back seat of the taxicab. She giggled and told him that she had had a long lunch with Christine. He laughed a little uncomfortably (somebody was standing by him while he was on the phone—she could always tell), and he said, "I thought you had a big presentation Monday?"

She replied, "Well, you're in luck. I'll have to go in to work tomorrow to finish it up. You can spend the day with your favorite person."

He asked, "Oh, and who is that?"

"Bret!" she roared. "Bret is your favorite person."

"Okay, well, I really have to go. I'll give you a call when I get home," he said trying to get off the phone and save face in front of whomever he was trying to impress.

"Why do you pick up the phone if you can't talk? You know it's me. You have Caller ID at the firm, fool," she asked him in a taunting voice.

"Okay, great. Talk to you then." Then he hung up the phone.

Bret did call her later that night—at around 10:00. "I'm just going to chalk up that phone call to a little too much wine," he states matter-of-factly.

"Bret, I meant the things I said. Sure, I had a few glasses of wine over a five-hour period, but I know what I said, and I meant what I said," Tara replies. She had taken a couple of aspirin and drunk a big bottle of water since arriving home. She felt fine.

"So, how was your friend?" Bret asks.

"Why would you change the subject? Don't you care that I'm upset?" she said.

"I just don't know what you're mad about. I don't know what more you want from me. Everything was going great, and you have lunch and hear that your friend is engaged, and all of a sudden you're on my case," Bret says.

"Yeah. It does bug me that other couples are getting married while we're in limbo," Tara explains.

"Tara, no guy proposes that fast. That's just crazy."

Tara shoots back, "Well, he did. And I never told you this, but that guy Patrick that I was seeing before I started dating you is also getting married."

"Well, you told me yourself what a weirdo he was," Bret replied.

"I'm thirty-one years old. I want to get married. I have been very honest with you about that since the beginning."

"Listen, I want to get married someday, too. But I'm not going to get married just because everybody else is. I don't want to make a mistake."

"Oh, so you think marrying me would be a mistake?" Tara asked

"That's not what I said. But things are going to great with us. Let's just enjoy ourselves and see what happens. You know that I love you. And I wouldn't be with you if I didn't see a future."

Tara thought this sounded pretty promising. She didn't want to do anything rash. Maybe things were salvageable. "Okay. But I just don't want to waste my time."

"Tara, you need to do what you need to do. I, for one, don't think this is a waste of time. I don't know what more I have to do to make you know that I am committed. I've introduced you to my family. You know all my friends. We've been on vacation together. You need to understand that that is big stuff for me. And for you to question my motives is really pretty sad."

"I'm sorry. I didn't mean it. Listen, let's just forget about this for now. I was just freaked out with this wedding coming up. Which reminds me, you're still going with me, aren't you?"

"When is it again?"

Tara bit her tongue. She had told him about twenty times when the wedding was. Obviously, it wasn't important enough for him to remember.

"The weekend of the twentieth."

"Oh. It's a whole-weekend thing?"

"Well, I would like to make a weekend out of it."

"When is the actual wedding?"

Tara took a deep breath. It was do-or-die time. She had given Bret so many chances. This was the last straw. You would think after her reading him the riot act on his inability to truly commit, that he would just do what *she* wanted to do for once. But no, he was so selfish. He felt so sure that she would never leave that he was willing to push his own agenda yet again.

She remembered *The List*. She remembered The Alarm. She obviously hadn't sounded The Alarm, and there was nothing she could do. She knew that she was at a crossroads. Why on earth would she want to bring Bret to a wedding? Even if he broke down and stayed for the weekend, she would be in the same place Sunday night. He would figure that the long weekend earned him time away from her.

"Listen, Bret, this just isn't working for me. Maybe you don't know what you want out of life but I do. I just want to be done with this."

"I just wanted to know how many days I needed to be up there!"

"This isn't about you. This is about me. You aren't what I want. And you really have never been what I want. I'm not mad. I have to move on."

"I don't want to break up," he said.

"But I do. And I am. Goodbye, Bret. If you want to do something for me, please don't call me. Goodbye."

She hung up the phone. And she felt sad but empowered. She felt relieved that she had stopped the clock on a relationship that had the potential of wasting months or years of her life.

And now here Tara sits at Christine's wedding. She feels a little raw but ready to hit the ground running. She holds her head high and takes her seat—alone—in the fourth row from the front. She will be okay on her own for the ceremony. It will be a little uncomfortable at the reception. She doesn't know a soul. But still, she knows it is better to be alone than to waste her time on a man who doesn't want what she wants. And what she wants is marriage. She has reread *The*

List and has her "must haves" tucked into her wallet. If she can just focus on her goal, maybe she will be the bride at the next wedding.

Megan arrives at Barry's wedding and is delighted beyond belief. As the music swells, Megan turns around to see the beautiful bride walking down the aisle on her father's arm. Megan knows Barry a little bit through her ex-boyfriend Colin. The two men had been in ROTC together during college. But Barry, unlike many of Colin's other friends, wasn't part of "the gang" of men that Colin ran with. He seemed to have other interests and was very respectful of the fact that Colin had a serious girlfriend. Imagine Megan's shock when she learned that Barry and Peter were neighbors! When the invitation arrived, she recognized Barry's name. She hadn't seen him in a couple of years at least. Peter and Barry weren't best friends, but they had spent a fair amount of time together watching football games on Barry's big screen before their alarms sounded.

Megan figures that Colin will be at the wedding. But he probably doesn't know that she is there. She is there, though—with her handsome fiancé and a sparkly diamond on her ring finger.

Christine looks dazzling in her mother's vintage 1963 silk-shantung Jackie Kennedy–style gown. Barry looks nervous but is beaming when Christine finally stands by his side at the end of the aisle. The ceremony is very simple. That is so Christine. After they are pronounced man and wife, they walk to the reception to the University of Minnesota fight song. That is so *not* Christine. But everybody smiles when they see how happy and carefree the bride is in the company of her new husband.

After the ceremony, Tara stands awkwardly in the reception tent, waiting in line for a glass of champagne. She is thrilled when the bride herself comes up to her and hugs her. "I'm so happy for you," Tara says tearfully. She doesn't know why she is choked up. It's a mixture of happiness for her friend and apprehension about her own future.

"Thank you. So, what do you think of him?" Christine asked her, all business.

"You have a very handsome husband," Tara replies.

"I know that! I'm talking about Barry's brother, Alan. The best man."

"Oh, that's right. Well, I only saw the back of him, but that looked pretty good," Tara deadpans.

They both start laughing. Neither of them sees Alan approach with two glasses of champagne. He hands one to Tara.

"Tara, this is Alan. Alan, Tara," Christine says. She looks at them both with a very serious expression.

"Nice to meet you," Alan says as he shakes her hand.

There is an awkward silence.

"Alan works in the construction industry," Christine continues.

"Oh, that's cool," Tara says.

"He's a foreman," Christine continues.

"Okay, okay. Thanks, sis. I think we can take things from here. Your husband is waiting for you," Alan says.

Christine leaves reluctantly. Somehow she has forgotten that she is at a wedding—her wedding.

Alan and Tara make easy conversation. She starts by saying. "Wow, can you believe what a whirlwind romance this was?" pointing to Christine and Barry on the dance floor.

"Isn't it great? I knew from the minute that Barry met Christine he was going to marry her," Alan responds easily.

Tara is impressed. He sure doesn't seem to think—as Bret did—that there is anything weird about a fast courtship. They continue their conversation easily. He is hilarious, and it's obvious Christine has told him a lot about Tara. It's like they've known each other for years. He isn't exactly her type, but she knows what her "must haves" are. He is cute in his own way and he has a great physique. He seems very aware that Tara is at the wedding by herself and so he stays by her side. Christine doesn't have formal seating assignments, so Alan sits by Tara at dinner and she feels like she has a friend for the evening.

A sweet couple, Peter and Megan, sit by them. They talk about their upcoming move to Oklahoma. Tara notices they are engaged and has a nice quiet conversation with Megan about how it all went down. Their courtship also went by *The List*. Alan notices that she and Megan are engrossed in girl talk and good-naturedly talks to Peter. Finally, Alan says, "Okay ladies. What's the big conversation about?"

"I don't think I even want to know," Peter replied with a smile.

Megan leans into the table and says that her ex-boyfriend is at the wedding. Peter smiles at her. Tara fills in the juicy details that she has just learned from Megan. At Alan's request, they pointed him out. "Oh yeah. He's the guy who brought the stripper," Alan says plainly.

"Shut up!" Tara says, slapping Alan's arm.

"What? Check it out," he responds.

They scan the tent. Finally, they see a girl wearing fishnets and platform heels with an otherwise pretty (albeit short) sundress. Just then Colin comes up to the woman and puts his arm around her.

They all burst out laughing. Megan catches Colin's eye and waves coyly (with her left hand, of course). He looks like he is going to pass out. Instead, he just turns the other way.

Alan says that he met Colin at the bachelor party, and that actually, Colin's date Sharon, isn't a stripper—she's a "model."

"Aren't they all," Tara says, laughing.

As the party goes on, everybody agrees that Christine and Barry's wedding is a success. Just when Tara is starting to think that Alan is flawed because he doesn't have a serious side, he surprises her with the toast he gives to the newlyweds: "A few months ago, Barry called me and told me that he had met someone. What he didn't have to tell me was that he was going to marry this lady. I could tell in his voice. I didn't even have to see him to know that he was in love. Once we met Christine, we fell for her too. She is smart, funny, successful, and as beautiful on the inside as she is on the outside. If everybody could be as happy as Barry and Christine, the world would be a much better place. To Barry and Christine."

"To Barry and Christine," the crowd toasts.

A few hours later, Barry and Christine depart on a pontoon boat to stay at the inn on the other side of the lake. They will see everybody at a brunch the next day. Megan and Peter had departed an hour earlier to get back to the city. Colin and "the model" are sloppily slow-dancing in the middle of the tent. She is clutching the bouquet that she caught a few hours before. Colin thinks that this girl could be the one for him. He is going to surprise her with a key to his apartment and an invitation to move in with him.

Tara tells Alan that it was nice to meet him as he walks her toward her car. She doesn't want to wreck a good thing by trying to cling to Alan any longer. She brought a bag in case she decided to stay overnight, but there isn't a hotel room left in town.

"Well, this was great. I'd like to get your phone number so we can get together," Alan says.

"Yes. I'd love that," she says.

"I'll give you a call tomorrow; maybe we can catch dinner on Tuesday."

"That sounds like a plan," she says. They hug tightly. She likes how it feels.

"Listen, why don't you stay? You can have my room, and I'll crash with my cousin," Alan suggests.

"Really?" Tara asks.

"Seriously. It's only ten o'clock. We can go back to the hotel bar and see Christine and Barry. I know darned well that they are still up for some fun. Barry told me that they weren't ready for the party to end. Neither am I. What do you say?"

"Okay. But I'm sleeping in your room, and you're sleeping in Chad's room. Got it?"

"How dare you question me? From what I hear, I'm the biggest gentleman to cross your doorstep in a long time," he smiles.

Tara laughs heartily. She's not concerned about what he may have learned from Christine about her dating history. She knows that if he is a List Man, it won't matter. She agrees with the plan. They collect her bag and ride to the hotel together. He reaches for her hand and it feels right. She hears her cell phone ringing in her purse. She drops his hand and digs her phone out of her purse. She stares at the number. It's Bret. She turns it off without answering.

"Everything okay?" he asks.

"Everything is great. Must have been a wrong number," she says. She reaches for Alan's hand.

Tara has a strong feeling that she is embarking on what *The List* calls a "never-ending date." Alan has checked three boxes in four hours. And the night is still young.

The List

Here is *The List* again—rip this page out, put it in your wallet and hold it close to your heart. Good luck! We would love to hear any stories of successful courtships in which the man completed all the items on *The List* within thirty days or less.

Please visit our Web site, at ✍ *www.thelistformarriage.com*.

1. He makes the first move.
2. He calls you within twenty-four to forty-eight hours to set up a first date.
3. He makes the first date easy and fun.
4. He calls you within twenty-four hours to set up subsequent dates—they are easy, fun, and one-on-one.
5. He wants to talk to you every day and wants to spend all his free time with you.
6. He demonstrates unconditional loyalty.
7. He talks about marrying you in concrete terms and proposes—or lets you know his intentions.

And, most importantly, all of these things will happen in thirty days or less.

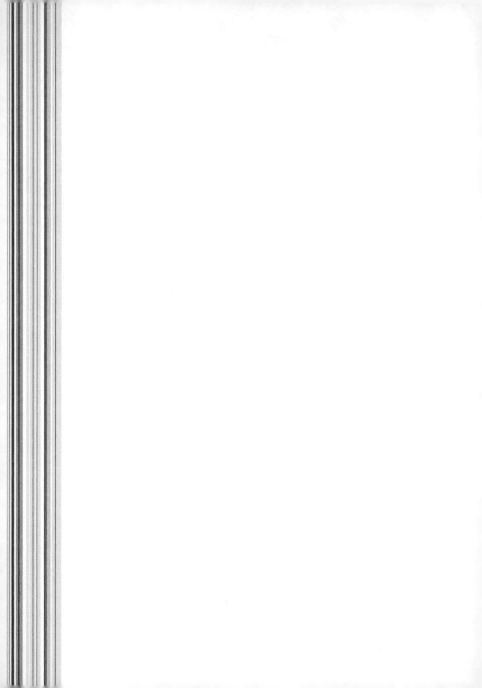

Index

About the Authors

MARY CORBETT and SHEILA CORBETT KIHNE are fiery sisters who share a passion for telling other people what to do.

After years of coaching friends through happy courtships that resulted in happy marriages—while watching other friends struggle in the singles scene or in the wrong long-term relationships—they wrote *The List*.

Mary lives in Alpharetta, Georgia, with her husband Jon and their children Holly and William. Sheila lives in Eden Prairie, Minnesota, with her husband Todd and daughters Jane and Kathleen.

The List is their first book.